CCNP Security (SCOR) Exam Prep

+400 Practice Questions

1st Edition

www.versatileread.com

Document Control

Proposal Name	:	CCNP Security (SCOR) Exam Prep: +400 Practice Questions
Document Edition	:	1st
Document Release Date	:	11th June 2024
Reference	:	SCOR – 350-701
VR Product Code	:	20241902SCOR

Feedback:
If you have any comments regarding the quality of this book or otherwise alter it to better suit your needs, you can contact us through email at info@versatileread.com

Please make sure to include the book's title and ISBN in your message.

About the Contributors:

Nouman Ahmed Khan

AWS/Azure/GCP-Architect, CCDE, CCIEx5 (R&S, SP, Security, DC, Wireless), CISSP, CISA, CISM, CRISC, ISO27K-LA is a Solution Architect working with a global telecommunication provider. He works with enterprises, mega-projects, and service providers to help them select the best-fit technology solutions. He also works as a consultant to understand customer business processes and helps select an appropriate technology strategy to support business goals. He has more than eighteen years of experience working with global clients. One of his notable experiences was his tenure with a large managed security services provider, where he was responsible for managing the complete MSSP product portfolio. With his extensive knowledge and expertise in various areas of technology, including cloud computing, network infrastructure, security, and risk management, Nouman has become a trusted advisor for his clients.

Abubakar Saeed

Abubakar Saeed is a trailblazer in the realm of technology and innovation. With a rich professional journey spanning over twenty-nine years, Abubakar has seamlessly blended his expertise in engineering with his passion for transformative leadership. Starting humbly at the grassroots level, he has significantly contributed to pioneering the Internet in Pakistan and beyond. Abubakar's multifaceted experience encompasses managing, consulting, designing, and implementing projects, showcasing his versatility as a leader.

His exceptional skills shine in leading businesses, where he champions innovation and transformation. Abubakar stands as a testament to the power of visionary leadership, heading operations, solutions design, and integration. His emphasis on adhering to project timelines and exceeding customer expectations has set him apart as a great leader. With an unwavering commitment to adopting technology for operational simplicity and enhanced efficiency, Abubakar Saeed continues to inspire and drive change in the industry.

Dr. Fahad Abdali

Dr. Fahad Abdali is an esteemed leader with an outstanding twenty-year track record in managing diverse businesses. With a stellar educational background, including a bachelor's degree from the prestigious NED University of Engineers & Technology and a Ph.D. from the University of Karachi, Dr. Abdali epitomizes academic excellence and continuous professional growth.

Dr. Abdali's leadership journey is marked by his unwavering commitment to innovation and his astute understanding of industry dynamics. His ability to navigate intricate challenges has driven growth and nurtured organizational triumph. Driven by a passion for excellence, he stands as a beacon of inspiration within the business realm. With his remarkable leadership skills, Dr. Fahad Abdali continues to steer businesses toward unprecedented success, making him a true embodiment of a great leader.

Umaima Maqsood

Umaima Maqsood is a versatile professional with expertise in technical content development and proficiency across diverse domains, notably cloud computing. With a focus on Amazon Web Services (AWS) Cloud Practitioner, AWS Advanced Networking, and AWS Machine Learning, she brings a wealth of knowledge to her work. Detail-oriented and analytically driven, Umaima thrives in collaborative environments, demonstrating a commitment to delivering excellence.

Table of Contents

About CCNP Security (SCOR) Certification

Implementing and Operating Cisco Security Core Technologies (SCOR) – Exam: 350-701

Introduction

The Implementing and Operating Cisco Security Core Technologies (SCOR 350-701) certification is the "CORE" certification for the CCNP Security and CCIE Security certifications. The CCNP-SCOR course helps you prepare for the Cisco CCNP Security and CCIE Security certifications and a few other expert-level security certifications. Bu completing this course, you can become an expert in the skills and technologies needed to implement core Cisco security solutions and provide advanced threat protection against cybersecurity attacks.

This course will thoroughly cover network security, cloud and content, endpoint protection, secure network access, visibility, and enforcement. It will provide comprehensive hands-on experience with Cisco Firepower, Next-Generation Firewall, and Cisco Adaptive Security Appliance (ASA) Firewall and establish access control rules, mail policies, and 802.1X Authentication. You will gain some hands-on experience with the threat detection features of Cisco Stealthwatch Enterprise and Cisco Stealthwatch Cloud.

Networking

Computer Networking is the way of conveying and exchanging data between nodes over a shared medium in an information system. Computer networking connects devices and endpoints on a Local Area Network (LAN) such as the internet or a private Wide Area Network (WAN). This is a necessary function for service providers, businesses, and consumers worldwide to share resources, use or provide services, and communicate. Everything from phone calls to text messaging to streaming video to the Internet of Things (IoT) is made easier via networking.

Networking is a combination of a network's design, construction, and use and the operation, management, and maintenance of the network

infrastructure, software, and policies. The skill level required to operate a network is related to its complexity. A large enterprise, for instance, may have thousands of nodes and extensive security requirements, such as end-to-end encryption, prompting the supervision of specialized network administrators. In a nutshell, networking technology has revolutionized the world and created a new arena for the overall development of all regions.

Security

Network security is a broad concept that encompasses a wide range of technologies, devices, and processes. In brief, it is a set of rules and configurations designed to protect the confidentiality, integrity, and accessibility of computer networks and data through the use of both software and hardware technologies. Regardless of magnitude, industry, or infrastructure, every organization requires network security solutions to protect it from the ever-increasing surroundings of cyber threats.

Currently, network infrastructure is complex with an ever-changing threat environment and attackers constantly looking for and exploiting vulnerabilities. These vulnerabilities can exist in various contexts, including users, devices, data, applications, and locations. As a result, many network security management tools and applications are currently in practice to address individual threats and exploits. These security measures are significant as a few minutes of the outage may cause widespread disruption and massive damage to an organization's baseline and reputation.

Cisco Certifications

Cisco Systems, Inc. is a global technology leader specializing in networking and communications products and services. The company is probably well known for its business switching and routing products, which direct data, voice, and video traffic across networks around the globe.

Cisco certifications are widely recognized and valuable certifications that an IT infrastructure professional can acquire. Cisco certification training courses are helpful when you need to succeed, whether you are preparing for your CCNA, CCNP, or CCENT exams.

Cisco's training and certification programs have been revamped to address today's dynamic technologies and to enable students, engineers, and software developers to succeed in the industry's most critical roles.

CCNP Security Certification

The CCNP Security certification is one of the most reputable in the industry. You must pass two examinations to achieve the CCNP Security Certification.

1. The required Security CORE (SCOR) exam, which contains Core security technologies (this course).
2. The Security Concentration exam (choose one) is your own so that you can tailor your certification to your technical area of interest.

Following are the CCNP Security Concentration exams:

- Securing Networks with Cisco Firepower (SNCF 300-710)
- Implementing and Configuring Cisco Identity Services Engine (SISE 300-715)
- Securing Email with Cisco Email Security Appliance (SESA 300-720)
- Securing the Web with Cisco Web Security Appliance (SWSA 300-725)
- Implementing Secure Solutions with Virtual Private Networks (SVPN 300-730)
- Automating Cisco Security Solutions (SAUTO 300-735)

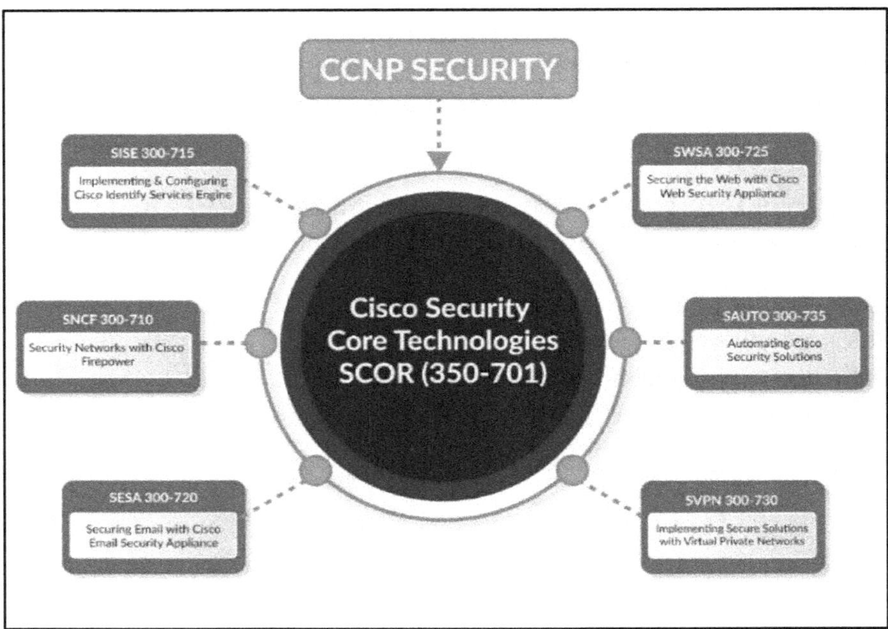

Why Should One Do CCNP?

A Cisco Certified Network Professional (CCNP) certification validates your competence in designing, deploying, and troubleshooting LAN and WAN networks. You will also be identified as a person who can collaborate with experts on challenges involving advanced security, wireless, voice, and video solutions.

CCNP certification is appropriate for those with at least one year of networking experience. Individuals who earn the certification have valuable skillsets required in enterprise professions such as network engineer, systems engineer, support engineer, network technician, etc. Before attempting the CCNP, you must first get CCNA certification.

What is SCOR?

SCOR is the mandatory Cisco Security "Core" exam for CCNP and CCIE Security certifications. SCOR 350-701 course has laid the base for a candidate interested in delving into the field of Cisco network security. The course addresses network security, cloud security, content security, endpoint protection and detection, secure network access, and visibility and enforcement. Suppose you pass the SCOR 350-701 exam. In that case, you

will have established the base for a career in network security and the potential to gain expertise in various areas and technologies.

How Does CCNP-SCOR Help?

CCNP-SCOR certification is a de facto standard in the network security industry, which helps you boost your career in the following ways:

- Learn best practices for implementing core security technologies and gaining hands-on experience with Cisco security solutions
- Prepare for the Cisco Security Core Technologies Implementing and Operating Exam (350-701 SCOR)
- Meet the requirements for professional and expert-level security roles
- Earn 64 Continuing Education credits toward recertification

Scope for CCNP-SCOR

Certified CCNP Security experts have a promising future. The retooled Cisco CCNP Certification has proven far more rewarding than the prior CCNA and CCNP certifications. The new curricula exceed individuals' professional expertise. As an outcome, there are plenty more career opportunities and attractive benefits for the certified CCNP - SCOR.

Who Should Enroll?

- Cisco integrators and partners
- Consulting systems engineers
- Network administrators, designers, engineers, and managers
- Security engineers
- Systems engineers
- Technical solution architects

Benefits of CCNP

Obtaining CCNP Security certification offers numerous benefits, including:

Enhanced Career Opportunities: CCNP-certified professionals are in high demand as organizations increasingly prioritize network security.

Industry Recognition: CCNP Security certification is globally recognized as a benchmark for network security expertise.

Skill Validation: CCNP certification validates your skills in designing, implementing, and managing Cisco network security solutions.

Career Advancement: CCNP-certified professionals often receive promotions and salary increases due to their specialized skills and expertise.

Access to Exclusive Resources: Cisco provides access to exclusive resources, including training materials, communities, and events, to support CCNP-certified professionals in their career development.

Prerequisites

One should have the following knowledge and skills to benefit from this course fully:

- Equivalent skills and knowledge gained in the Implementing and Administering Cisco Solutions (CCNA®) v1.0 course
- Knowledge of Ethernet and TCP/IP networking
- Knowledge of the Windows operating system
- Working understanding of Cisco IOS networking concepts and protocols
- Familiarity with the fundamentals of networking security concepts

Exam Information

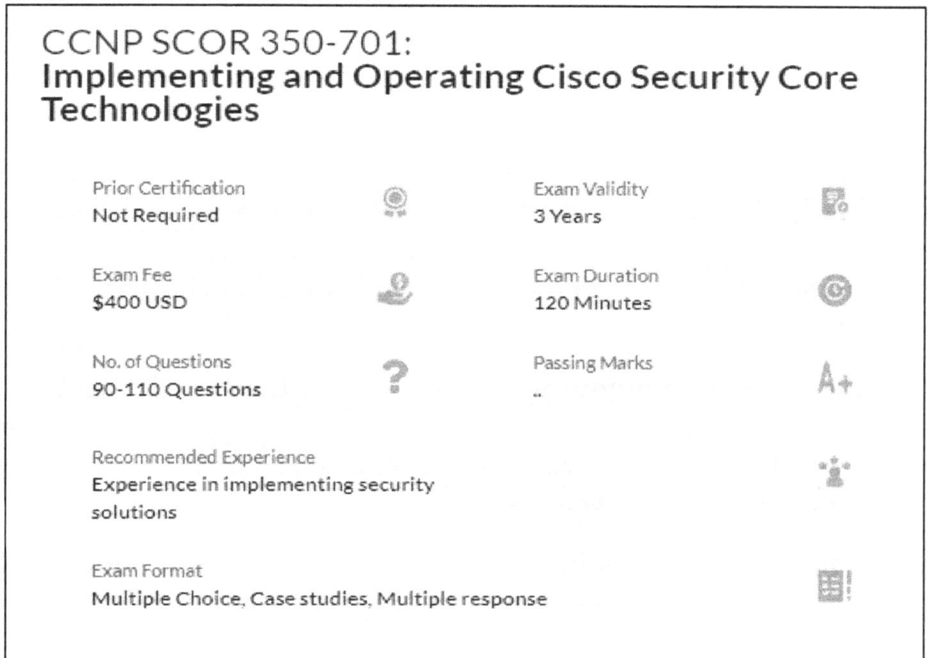

CCNP SCOR 350-701:
Implementing and Operating Cisco Security Core Technologies
Prior Certification
Not Required
Exam Validity
3 Years
Exam Fee
$400 USD
Exam Duration
120 Minutes
No. of Questions
90-110 Questions
Passing Marks
..
A+
Recommended Experience
Experience in implementing security solutions
Exam Format
Multiple Choice, Case studies, Multiple response

CCNP Exam Preparation Pointers

Preparing for CCNP exams requires dedication, focus, and effective study strategies to ensure success. Here are some pointers to help you prepare effectively for your CCNP exams:

Understand Exam Topics: Review the exam blueprint and study objectives provided by Cisco to understand the topics covered in the exam. Focus your study efforts on mastering these topics.

Utilize Official Study Materials: Use official Cisco study materials, such as textbooks, study guides, and practice exams, to supplement your learning. These materials are designed to align with the exam objectives and provide comprehensive coverage of exam topics.

Hands-on Practice: Gain practical experience with Cisco networking technologies by setting up lab environments and working through hands-on

exercises. Practice configuring routers, switches, and other network devices to reinforce your understanding of key concepts.

Enroll in Training Courses: Consider enrolling in instructor-led training courses offered by Cisco or authorized training partners. These courses provide structured learning experiences led by experienced instructors and often include hands-on labs and interactive exercises.

Join Study Groups: Join online forums or study groups to connect with other CCNP candidates, share study resources, and discuss exam topics. Collaborating with peers can provide valuable insights and support during the exam preparation process.

Practice Time Management: Develop effective time management skills to ensure you can answer all questions within the allotted time during the exam. Practice taking timed practice exams to simulate the exam environment and improve your pacing.

Stay Updated: Stay informed about updates to exam content, study materials, and exam policies by regularly checking the Cisco Certification website and official Cisco forums. Be prepared to adjust your study plan accordingly based on any changes.

Job Opportunities with CCNP Certifications

Earning a Cisco Certified Network Professional (CCNP) certification opens up a wide range of job opportunities in the field of networking and IT infrastructure. As a highly respected certification, CCNP validates the skills and expertise required to plan, implement, verify, and troubleshoot complex network solutions.

Here are some of the job opportunities available to individuals with CCNP certifications:

Network Engineer: Network engineers design, implement, and maintain computer networks for organizations. With a CCNP certification, network engineers are equipped to handle advanced networking tasks such as configuring routers and switches, optimizing network performance, and troubleshooting network issues.

Network Administrator: Network administrators are responsible for managing and maintaining an organization's network infrastructure. With a CCNP certification, network administrators have the skills needed to oversee network operations, monitor network performance, and ensure network security.

Systems Engineer: Systems engineers design and implement complex IT systems, including network infrastructure, servers, and storage solutions. With a CCNP certification, systems engineers are well-prepared to design and deploy robust network architectures that meet the needs of modern businesses.

Network Consultant: Network consultants provide expert advice and guidance to organizations looking to improve their network infrastructure. With a CCNP certification, network consultants can assess existing network environments, recommend solutions for optimization and security, and assist with implementation and troubleshooting.

Security Engineer: Security engineers specialize in protecting organizations' networks and data from cyber threats. With a CCNP Security certification, security engineers have the skills required to implement and manage security solutions such as firewalls, VPNs, and intrusion detection systems.

Wireless Engineer: Wireless engineers design, deploy, and optimize wireless networks for organizations. With a CCNP Wireless certification, wireless engineers can configure and troubleshoot wireless networks, optimize network performance, and ensure security and compliance.

Cloud Engineer: Cloud engineers design, implement, and manage cloud-based solutions for organizations. With a CCNP Cloud certification, cloud engineers have the skills needed to integrate on-premises networks with cloud services, manage cloud resources, and ensure data security and compliance.

Data Center Engineer: Data center engineers design and maintain data center infrastructure, including servers, storage systems, and networking equipment. With a CCNP Data Center certification, data center engineers

can deploy and manage data center networks, optimize performance, and ensure high availability and reliability.

VoIP Engineer: VoIP engineers specialize in designing, implementing, and managing Voice over IP (VoIP) systems for organizations. With a CCNP Voice certification, VoIP engineers have the skills required to configure VoIP networks, troubleshoot call quality issues and ensure reliable communication services.

IT Manager: IT managers oversee the planning, implementation, and management of IT systems and infrastructure within organizations. With a CCNP certification, IT managers have the technical expertise needed to make informed decisions about network architecture, security, and performance optimization.

Demand for CCNP Certification in 2024

As we move further into the digital age, the demand for skilled IT professionals continues to rise, and certifications like Cisco Certified Network Professional (CCNP) remain highly sought after by employers. In 2024, the demand for CCNP-certified professionals is expected to remain strong, driven by several key factors:

Increasing Complexity of Networks: With the rapid evolution of technology, networks are becoming increasingly complex. Organizations require skilled professionals who can design, implement, and manage complex network infrastructures to support their operations. CCNP certification validates the expertise needed to tackle these challenges effectively.

Growing Importance of Network Security: As cyber threats become more sophisticated and prevalent, network security has become a top priority for organizations across industries. CCNP Security certification equips professionals with the knowledge and skills to implement robust security measures and protect networks from cyber attacks.

Expansion of Cloud Computing: The adoption of cloud computing continues to grow, with many organizations migrating their IT infrastructure to cloud platforms like AWS, Azure, and Google Cloud. CCNP

Cloud certification prepares professionals to design, deploy, and manage cloud-based networks, making them indispensable in today's cloud-centric environment.

Emergence of New Technologies: Technologies like 5G, Internet of Things (IoT), and artificial intelligence (AI) are reshaping the networking landscape. CCNP-certified professionals who stay updated with the latest advancements in technology are well-positioned to leverage these technologies to drive innovation and business growth.

Remote Workforce and Hybrid IT Environments: The shift towards remote work and hybrid IT environments has accelerated the demand for network professionals who can ensure seamless connectivity and collaboration across distributed networks. CCNP certification provides professionals with the skills to design and manage network infrastructures that support remote work and digital collaboration.

Industry Recognition and Validation: CCNP certification is widely recognized and respected in the IT industry. Employers value CCNP-certified professionals for their demonstrated expertise and commitment to excellence. As a result, CCNP certification remains a valuable asset for individuals looking to advance their careers in networking.

Practice Questions

1. What are two examples of cloud computing services mentioned in the text?

A) Data centers and co-location

B) Managed hosting and IaaS

C) PaaS and SQL injection

D) Trojans and phishing

2. Which of the following is NOT listed as a common on-premises threat?

A) SQL injection

B) DDoS attacks

C) Ransomware

D) Session hijacking

3. According to the text, what is the number one asset for any company?

A) Data

B) Systems

C) Employees

D) Trade secrets

4. What type of attack involves an attacker intercepting traffic between a user and a web resource?

A) DoS attack

B) Session hijacking

C) SQL injection

D) Rootkit attack

5. What is the primary goal of a phishing attack?

A) Disrupting network services

B) Stealing sensitive user data

C) Intercepting web server traffic

D) Modifying firmware

6. Which attack method involves injecting malicious code into strings destined for storage in a database?

A) DoS attack

B) DDoS attack

C) SQL injection

D) XSS attack

7. What type of malware is designed to act as surveillance, monitoring a system's usage?

A) Viruses

B) Spyware

C) Trojans

D) Ransomware

8. What is the purpose of a crypter in malware?

A) To propagate malware to other systems

B) To erase data on the victim's system

C) To encrypt and obscure the malware code

D) To generate pop-ups to deceive users

9. Which attack method involves flooding a network or system with requests to disrupt legitimate users?

A) Phishing attack

B) SQL injection

C) DoS attack

D) Rootkit attack

10. What is the main characteristic of a virus, according to the text?

A) It requires human interaction to start the infection

B) It infects systems by exploiting vulnerabilities

C) It primarily targets hardware components

D) It spreads automatically over a network

11. How do nation-state actors differ from other attackers, according to the text?

A) They have limited budgets and resources

B) They primarily target individual users

C) They tend to be less skilled in cyber-attacks

D) They have unlimited budgets and resources

12. What is the primary effect of a DoS attack?

A) Stealing sensitive user data

B) Intercepting web server traffic

C) Disabling and denying service to legitimate users

D) Executing malicious code on a victim's system

13. What type of attack involves injecting malicious JavaScript into a website or web application?

A) SQL injection

B) DoS attack

C) XSS attack

D) Rootkit attack

14. Which of the following is NOT a type of XSS attack?

A) Cross-site scripting

B) DOM-based XSS

C) Reflected XSS

D) Stored XSS

15. Which of the following will you use for your organization as a collection of industry standards and achieve best practices to manage security risks?

A) CERT/cc

B) NIST Cybersecurity Framework

C) ISO Cybersecurity Framework

D) MITRE

16. What is the purpose of ARP spoofing in a man-in-the-middle attack?

A) To corrupt the Domain Name System's resolver cache

B) To flood the network with ARP misinformation

C) To intercept and change the operating system processes

D) To redirect traffic to the attacker's device

17. Which attack method involves diverting the user to the attacker's website by corrupting the DNS resolver cache?

A) DNS spoofing

B) Wi-Fi eavesdropping

C) Session hijacking

D) SSL stripping

18. How does SSL stripping downgrade the communication between the client and the server?

A) By flooding the network with requests

B) By intercepting and changing the operating system processes

C) By corrupting the DNS resolver cache

D) By converting HTTPS URLs to HTTP links

19. What is the primary goal of a dropper in malware?

A) To intercept and change the operating system processes

B) To encrypt and obscure the malware code

C) To install malware on the victim's system

D) To flood the network with requests

20. What type of Trojan is used to gain full control of a system?

A) Click-fraud Trojan

B) Data-hiding Trojan

C) Remote access Trojan (RAT)

D) E-banking Trojan

21. How does a DoS attack differ from a DDoS attack?

A) A DoS attack involves multiple machines attacking a single host

B) A DDoS attack involves flooding a network with requests

C) A DoS attack targets a single host, while a DDoS attack targets multiple hosts

D) A DDoS attack is typically executed on a local network

22. What type of attack occurs when an attacker floods a network with ICMP requests?

A) Phishing attack

B) SQL injection

C) DoS attack

D) XSS attack

23. What is the primary purpose of hashing in cryptography?

A) To encrypt sensitive data

B) To verify data integrity

C) To authenticate users

D) To generate random keys

24. Which command is used on Cisco devices to generate a hash for verification?

A) encrypt /sha256

B) verify /md5

C) generate /sha1

D) hash /sha512

25. What is the main function of encryption in cryptography?

A) To verify data integrity

B) To authenticate users

C) To convert plaintext to cipher text

D) To generate digital signatures

26. In asymmetric encryption, how many keys are used for encryption and decryption?

A) One secret key

B) Two secret keys

C) One public key and one private key

D) Two public keys

27. What is the purpose of Public Key Infrastructure (PKI) in cryptography?

A) To encrypt data with a single key

B) To authenticate users with biometrics

C) To manage digital certificates and keys

D) To perform secure network routing

28. Which cryptographic protocol is commonly used for HTTPS to enable secure web communication?

A) TLS/SSL

B) IPsec

C) SSH

D) VPN

29. What is NAT-T in cryptography used for?

A) To bypass firewalls

B) To encrypt network traffic

C) To establish VPN connections over NAT devices

D) To authenticate users in remote access VPNs

30. What is the purpose of pre-shared keys in cryptography?

A) To authenticate users in PKI

B) To encrypt sensitive data in transit

C) To establish secure connections between devices

D) To store encrypted passwords in databases

31. How does certificate-based encryption work?

A) By using symmetric keys for encryption

B) By generating random keys for each session

C) By using digital certificates issued by a Certificate Authority

D) By authenticating users with biometric data

32. What type of VPN securely connects two remote LAN sites?

A) Remote access VPN

B) sVTI-based VPN

C) Site-to-site VPN

D) Client-based VPN

33. Which VPN type is commonly used by individual users to connect to a remote LAN?

A) Site-to-site VPN

B) sVTI-based VPN

C) Remote access VPN

D) Client-based VPN

34.What is the primary advantage of using DMVPN?

A) It requires static configuration on all devices

B) It supports only hub-and-spoke topologies

C) It enables direct communication between spokes without passing traffic through the hub

D) It encrypts data using SSL/TLS

35.Which configuration method does FlexVPN use to support various IPsec VPN types?

A) Cryptomaps

B) sVTI

C) IKEv1

D) IKEv2

36.Which Cisco module provides advanced endpoint protection across control points?

A) Cisco Secure Firewall

B) Cisco Secure Endpoint (SEP)

C) Cisco Umbrella Roaming

D) Identity Services Engine (ISE)

37.What is the main purpose of Security Intelligence (SI) in an organization?

A) To gather and analyze threat information

B) To authenticate users

C) To encrypt network traffic

D) To provide network routing

38. Which Cisco team is responsible for collecting and sharing security intelligence?

A) Cisco Umbrella

B) Cisco Talos Security Intelligence

C) Cisco Secure Endpoint

D) Cisco Identity Services Engine (ISE)

39.How does Cisco Talos contribute to enhancing security posture?

A) By providing cloud management console

B) By offering endpoint protection

C) By collecting, authoring, and sharing security intelligence

D) By integrating with identity services

40. Which Cisco appliance analyzes emails for spam, phishing, and malware?

A) Cisco Secure Firewall

B) Cisco Web Security Appliance (WSA)

C) Cisco Secure Endpoint (SEP)

D) Cisco Identity Services Engine (ISE)

41. What type of VPN enables direct communication between spokes without passing traffic through the hub?

A) DMVPN

B) Site-to-site VPN

C) Remote access VPN

D) Client-based VPN

42. Which VPN type uses a web browser portal for access?

A) DMVPN

B) sVTI-based VPN

C) Remote access VPN

D) Client-based VPN

43. What is the primary advantage of sVTI-based VPNs over cryptomap-based VPNs?

A) They support multicast and routing protocols

B) They require less configuration and management overhead

C) They provide stronger encryption algorithms

D) They use public keys for authentication

44. What is the primary function of the policy-map command in configuring an sVTI-based IPsec tunnel?

A) To shape traffic

B) To encrypt traffic

C) To authenticate users

D) To configure access control lists

45. Which of the following security models Google created resembles the zero-trust concept?

A) TrustSec
B) BeyondCorp
C) Duo
D) pxGrid

46. IPFIX was created on the basis of ______________.

A) NetFlow v9
B) NetFlow v5
C) Flexible NetFlow
D) None of the above

47. Which of the following term refers to the potential danger to a resource or asset?

A) Exploit

B) Threat

C) Vulnerability

D) None of the above

48. Which of the following term refers to the weakness in a system's code, design, or implementation?

A) Exploit

B) Threat

C) Vulnerability

D) None of the above

49. What is the primary objective of cloud patch management?

A) Improve system performance

B) Keep cloud-based systems updated with the latest security patches

C) Increase system storage capacity

D) Reduce network latency

50.Which cloud model involves sharing infrastructure among multiple organizations?

A) Public Cloud

B) Private Cloud

C) Hybrid Cloud

D) Community Cloud

51. What does SaaS stand for?

A) System as a Service

B) Software as a Service

C) Security as a Service

D) Storage as a Service

52. In a PaaS model, who is responsible for application patching?

A) Cloud provider

B) End customer

C) Third-party vendor

D) No one

53. Which NIST publication defines cloud computing and its essential characteristics?

A) NIST SP 800-53

B) NIST SP 800-145

C) NIST SP 500-322

D) NIST SP 800-30

54. What is the role of Cisco Cloudlock in cloud deployments?

A) Cloud access security broker

B) Data storage solution

C) Cloud service provider

D) Network performance optimizer

55. What does IaaS provide to customers?

A) On-demand access to software applications

B) On-demand access to cloud-hosted physical and virtual servers, storage, and networking

C) A complete platform for developing and managing applications

D) Access to development tools and services

56. What type of environment does a hybrid cloud involve?

A) Only public cloud resources

B) Only private cloud resources

C) A combination of public cloud and private on-premises resources

D) A community-shared environment

57.Which cloud service model has the customer only responsible for the data entered into the system?

A) SaaS

B) PaaS

C) IaaS

D) XaaS

58.What is a major benefit of public cloud distributed storage?

A) Reduced security risk

B) Increased physical security

C) Ease of scaling out

D) Lower costs

59.Which cloud model is recommended by Cisco for deploying critical applications and functions?

A) Public Cloud

B) Private Cloud

C) Hybrid Cloud

D) Community Cloud

60.In which cloud service model does the cloud provider handle operating system maintenance and below?

A) SaaS

B) PaaS

C) IaaS

D) XaaS

61. What percentage of IT organizations operate using hybrid cloud according to the text?

A) 50%

B) 62%

C) 72%

D) 82%

62.What is the primary benefit of the NIST 800-145 definition for cloud computing?

A) It reduces operational costs

B) It provides a standardized framework for defining cloud computing

C) It offers specific security solutions

D) It enhances performance

63. What does DevSecOps integrate into the CI/CD pipeline?

A) Development and operations

B) Security and operations

C) Development, security, and operations

D) Security and development

64. What is the main focus of private cloud security?

A) Security of multiple tenants

B) Security of a single customer's infrastructure

C) Security of public internet resources

D) Security of hybrid environments

65.What does cloud logging primarily help with?

A) Data storage optimization

B) Network speed improvement

C) Security and compliance monitoring

D) Reducing operational costs

66. Which Cisco solution helps with cloud patch management?

A) Cisco ISE

B) Cisco Cloudlock

C) Cisco Secure Workload

D) Cisco Nexus

67.What kind of infrastructure does a community cloud involve?

A) Infrastructure dedicated to a single organization

B) Infrastructure shared among multiple organizations with similar goals

C) Public internet infrastructure

D) Combination of private and public infrastructure

68.What is a workload in the context of Cisco Secure Workload?

A) A server or host with an IP address

B) A software application

C) A user's task

D) A data storage unit

69. What is the key feature of SaaS that differentiates it from other cloud service models?

A) User management

B) On-demand software application access

C) Infrastructure management

D) Development tools access

70.What does PaaS stand for?

A) Platform as a Service

B) Programming as a Service

C) Processing as a Service

D) Performance as a Service

71. Which type of cloud provides the highest level of control to the customer?

A) SaaS

B) PaaS

C) IaaS

D) Community Cloud

72.What is the main advantage of container orchestration?

A) Reduced costs

B) Automated deployment and management of containers

C) Improved physical security

D) Increased storage capacity

73.What does Cisco recommend for managing secrets in the CI/CD pipeline?

A) Storing them in plaintext

B) Encrypting them at rest

C) Using third-party storage solutions

D) Disabling secrets management

74.What is a significant benefit of using IaaS?

A) Faster application development

B) Comprehensive security measures

C) Reduced need for patch management

D) Simplified user access

75. What is one of the primary uses of cloud security assessments?

A) Enhancing data storage capacity

B) Reducing cloud service costs

C) Assessing the overall security posture of cloud infrastructure

D) Increasing network speed

76. What does the term "cloud-native applications" refer to?

A) Applications designed to run in traditional data centers

B) Applications developed to run in cloud environments

C) Applications for managing cloud resources

D) Applications hosted on private clouds

77.Which cloud model is characterized by allowing resources to scale up or down as needed by a single organization?

A) Public Cloud

B) Private Cloud

C) Community Cloud

D) Hybrid Cloud

78.What does the NIST SP 500-322 outline?

A) Cloud security guidelines

B) Cloud service models and deployment strategies

C) Application development standards

D) Network infrastructure requirements

79.Which security model allows the customer to have control over operating systems, applications, and data?

A) SaaS

B) PaaS

C) IaaS

D) NaaS

80.What is the purpose of a CASB solution like Cisco Cloudlock?

A) To provide cloud storage

B) To optimize network performance

C) To secure cloud environments

D) To develop applications

81.What kind of cloud does Cisco recommend for critical applications?

A) Public Cloud

B) Private Cloud

C) Hybrid Cloud

D) Community Cloud

82.What is a major challenge of hybrid cloud environments?

A) Limited scalability

B) Difficulty in managing security and monitoring solutions

C) High cost of deployment

D) Poor performance

83.What is the main benefit of using SaaS for organizations?

A) Full control over infrastructure

B) On-demand access to applications without managing the underlying infrastructure

C) Increased storage capacity

D) Enhanced security features

84.Which cloud service model is most suitable for organizations that want to develop and run applications without managing the underlying hardware?

A) SaaS

B) PaaS

C) IaaS

D) NaaS

85.How does Cisco Secure Workload help in application security?

A) By creating firewalls at the workload level

B) By providing cloud storage

C) By optimizing network performance

D) By offering development tools

86.What does SDLC stand for in the context of secure software development?

A) Software Development Life Cycle

B) System Design Life Cycle

C) Secure Data Life Cycle

D) Software Deployment Life Cycle

87.What does Cisco recommend for hybrid environment patch management?

A) Using multiple solutions

B) Using a single solution to track and patch across environments

C) Avoiding patching third-party applications

D) Manually tracking patches

88.What is a major benefit of cloud security assessments?

A) They increase the speed of the network

B) They enhance the visibility of the security posture

C) They reduce the cost of cloud services

D) They improve data storage capacity

89.Which feature does Cisco Secure Workload offer for disaster recovery?

A) Automated data backups

B) Data encryption

C) Compliance monitoring

D) Network traffic optimization

90. There is a vulnerability in the web application, but the attack is against the end users' browsers. Choose the correct vulnerability that defines this attack.

A) SQL Injection

B) XXE

C) XSS

D) HTML Injection

91. Which of the following is used to identify a vulnerability?
A) PSIRT
B) CVE
C) CVSS
D) All of the above

92. Which of the following term refers to the knowledge of an existing or becoming a known threat to any system, network, or asset?
A) Threat assessment
B) Exploit
C) Vulnerabilities
D) Threat intelligence

93. Which of the following terms refers to the tool, process, or technique to take advantage of a vulnerability in any system?
A) Searchsploit
B) Reverse Shell
C) Exploit
D) None of the above

94. Which of the following refers to an adverse event that can discontinue a business's services or threaten it in any way?
A) An IPS alert
B) An incident
C) A SIEM alert
D) A DLP alert

95. Which of the following is not a protocol in an IoT network or environment that is used for communication?

A) INSTEON

B) 802.1x

C) LoRaWAN

D) Zigbee

96. Which one of the following cloud models has all the phases of SDLC (System Development Life Cycle) and can use web portals, APIs (Application Programming Interfaces), or gateway software?

A) PaaS

B) SDLC containers

C) SaaS

D) None of the above

97. If an attacker steals the credentials of a router and changes its configuration. What does it impact?

A) Session keys

B) Integrity

C) Encryption

D) None of the above

98. Which of the following is impacted by a denial-of-service attack?

A) Confidentiality

B) Integrity

C) Availability

D) All of the above

99. Which type of hacker refers to the hacker who works for good causes?

A) Black hat

B) White hat

C) Gray hat

D) None of the above

100. Select one of the following that is not an example of ransomware.

A) Nyeta

B) Pyeta

C) WannaCry

D) Ret2Libc

E) Bad Rabbit

101. Which of the following terms refers to the way of documentation and preservation of the evidence from the time of cyber-forensics investigation to the time of presenting it to the court?

A) Best evidence

B) Faraday

C) Chain of custody

D) None of the above

102. Why are endpoint devices and people often targeted by attackers?

A) Due to their advanced security features

B) Because they are the most difficult targets

C) Because attackers exploit human trust weaknesses

D) Because they have complex encryption algorithms

103.How does Cisco Secure Endpoint protect endpoints from threats?

A) By providing network monitoring only

B) By encrypting all data traffic

C) By stopping known malware and monitoring activity

D) By blocking all inbound traffic

104.Which API facilitates the exchange of actionable data between systems in SDN?

A) Eastbound API

B) Southbound API

C) Northbound API

D) Westbound API

105.What is the role of the northbound API in SDN?

A) To deliver network configurations to devices

B) To integrate distributed computing network components

C) To facilitate management solutions for automation

D) To interact with the data plane of network devices

106.How does SDN differ from traditional networking?

A) SDN uses a centralized controller for network management

B) Traditional networking relies on distributed control elements

C) SDN provides better scalability but lower security

D) Traditional networking offers more flexibility in network configuration

107.What is the function of the southbound API in SDN?

A) To interact with the application and management plane

B) To communicate between controllers and switches

C) To facilitate automation and orchestration

D) To deliver network configurations to devices

108.How does DNAC assist in network provisioning?

A) By providing real-time traffic analysis

B) By integrating with external alert systems

C) By baselining network performance

D) By pushing intent-based configurations to devices

109.Which component sits at the top level of DNAC's architecture?

A) Cisco Identity Services Engine (ISE)

B) Open Platform, API Bound calls

C) Cisco Catalyst 9000 seed devices

D) Assurance engine

110.What role does machine learning play in DNAC's assurance feature?

A) It facilitates network provisioning

B) It provides real-time traffic analysis

C) It baselines network performance

D) It detects anomalies and alerts administrators

111.What is the primary advantage of using Python for network automation?

A) It is a compiled language

B) It requires extensive manual coding

C) It provides a dynamic typing system

D) It lacks support for external APIs

112.What is the purpose of the requests library in Python scripts?

A) To handle operating system commands

B) To manage JSON data

C) To interact with external APIs

D) To import Python libraries

113.How can Python scripts interact with Cisco Firepower appliances?

A) By executing shell commands

B) By using the Netmiko library

C) By directly accessing the device's operating system

D) By embedding API calls within the script

114.What is a potential security risk associated with hardcoded credentials in Python scripts?

A) Directory traversal attacks

B) Cross-site scripting (XSS)

C) SQL injection attacks

D) Credential theft

115.Which Python module can help sanitize user input in scripts?

A) ast

B) shlex

C) requests

D) sys

116.What is the purpose of the eastbound API in network integration?

A) To send data out to integrate with external systems

B) To define how the SDN controller interacts with the application plane

C) To facilitate communication between controllers and switches

D) To manage network configurations

117.How does Netmiko facilitate Python script interaction with network devices?

A) By providing SSH protocol implementation

B) By enabling REST API calls

C) By automating directory traversal

D) By sanitizing user inputs

118.Which Python library is based on Paramiko for SSH protocol implementation?

A) ast

B) requests

C) Netmiko

D) shlex

119.What is the purpose of the Open Platform, API Bound calls in DNAC's architecture?

A) To integrate with external alert systems

B) To manage network configurations

C) To facilitate interaction with external APIs

D) To provide real-time traffic analysis

120.How does DNAC assist in network troubleshooting?

A) By providing real-time traffic analysis

B) By detecting and alerting on anomalies

C) By managing network configurations

D) By baselining network performance

121.Which Python module is commonly used for parsing command-line parameters?

A) ast

B) requests

C) argparse

D) shlex

122. Which of the following types of cloud deployment models' cloud environment can be shared among different organizations?

A) IaaS

B) PaaS

C) Community cloud

D) None of the above

123.How does Cisco Secure Endpoint protect against threats?

A) By encrypting all network traffic

B) By providing real-time traffic analysis

C) By stopping known malware and monitoring activity

D) By allowing all inbound traffic

124. In which of the following attacks the attacker sends a request (packet) to a source (a random node in the network), and then that source replies with a response packet to the actual victim of the attacker?

A) Reflected DDoS

B) SYN flood

C) Direct DoS

D) Backtrack DoS

125. Various industry-wide initiatives to promote the security of software, applications, and web applications are led by which of the following non-profit organization?

A) OWASP

B) AppSec

C) CERT/cc

D) FIRST

126. Which of the following keys can be used only once?

A) ISAKMP

B) Multifactor key

C) OTP

D) None of the above

127. Which of the following clients can be used for remote access VPN, secure network access, and posture assessments with Cisco's Identity Services Engine?
A) DUO
B) AnyConnect
C) Tetration
D) Cisco SMA

128. Which ciphers use the same key for encryption and decryption?
A) Ciphertext
B) RSA

C) Asymmetric

D) Symmetric

129.How does Netmiko facilitate Python script interaction with network devices?

A) By automating directory traversal

B) By providing SSH protocol implementation

C) By enabling REST API calls

D) By sanitizing user inputs

130. Which of the following symmetric cipher uses one bit of the key stream at a time to encrypt the plaintext data? (It is also known as cipher digit stream.)
A) Block cipher
B) Stream cipher

C) Asymmetric cipher

D) None of the above

131. Which of the following is not a symmetric encryption algorithm?
A) RSA
B) AES

C) RC4

D) 3DES

132. Which of the following algorithms uses a negotiation method and establishment of a shared secret keying material (keys) between two devices over an untrusted network (usually the Internet)?
A) RC4
B) RSA

C) IKE

D) Diffie-Hellman

133. How does a CASB like Cisco Cloudlock help secure cloud applications?

A) By providing additional data storage

B) By offering network optimization

C) By monitoring and managing cloud application security and compliance

D) By developing cloud-native applications

134. Using PGP or S/MIME, John wants to send an encrypted email to Mike. Which of the following keys will John use for encryption?
A) Mike's public key
B) John's public key

C) Mike's private key

D) John's private key

135. Which of the following entities is responsible for creating and issuing digital certificates?

A) Certificate Authentication Server (CAS)

B) Certificate Authority (CA)

C) Certificate Registry (CR)

D) None of the above

136. Which of the following is a series of standards focused on the services and organization of the directories?

A) X.11

B) X.409

C) 802.1x

D) X.500

137.Which Python library is commonly used for interacting with web APIs?

A) ast

B) sys

C) requests

D) shlex

138. Inside a digital certificate, which of the following entities will be found? (Choose two)

A) DNS server IP address

B) FQDN

C) Public key

D) Default gateway

139. Select the format used to store the private and public keys using a password-based key (symmetric) to unlock the data whenever you want to access or use the keys?

A) PKCS #7

B) PKCS #10

C) PKCS #12

D) None of the above

140.What is the primary function of Netmiko in Python scripting?

A) To analyze network traffic

B) To provide SSH protocol implementation

C) To interact with web APIs

D) To sanitize user inputs

141.How does DNAC leverage machine learning for network assurance?

A) By automatically configuring network devices

B) By detecting and alerting on anomalies

C) By monitoring user activity

D) By optimizing network performance

142. Which of the following will you use to create network overlays?

A) VXLAN

B) VXWAN

C) SDN-Lane

D) None of the above

143.Which module in Python helps sanitize user inputs by processing abstract syntax trees?

A) requests

B) sys

C) ast

D) shlex

144. Which of the following tag represents a logical segment?

A) VXLAN Segment Identifier (VSID)

B) VXLAN Network Identifier (VNID)

C) Application Policy Infrastructure Controller (APIC)

D) ACI Network Identifier (ANID)

145. Which of the following terms refers to the network traffic between the containers, servers, and so on?

A) North-South traffic

B) Network overlays

C) Micro-segmentation

D) East-West traffic

146. Which of the following ranges of HTTP codes belongs to the successful HTTP transaction.

A) Messages in the range of 500

B) Messages in the range of 400

C) Messages in the range of 200

D) Messages in the range of 100

147. Which of the following APIs use XML exclusively?

A) REST

B) APIC

C) GraphQL

D) SOAP

148.Which module in Python helps sanitize user inputs by processing abstract syntax trees?

A) requests

B) sys

C) ast

D) shlex

149. Which of the following is the basis of OpenAPI Specification (OAS)? (It is also a modern framework of API documentation.)

A) REST

B) SOAP

C) Swagger

D) WSDL

150. RESTCONF interface is built around a few standardized requests. Which of the following requests are supported by it?

A) PATCH

B) PUT

C) GET

D) All of the above

151. The NETCONF standard defines which of the following structures to encode its messages?

A) XML

B) OWASP

C) RESTCONF

D) JSON

152. Which technology extension of NetFlow provides the ability to collect security information in one cache and traffic analysis in separate caches?

A) IPFIX

B) ISAKMP

C) TCP

D) ICMP

153. What technology does Cisco use to provide next-generation security products that offer protection throughout the attack continuum?

A) SNMP

B) NTP

C) FirePOWER

D) DHCP

154. What is the primary function of intrusion detection systems (IDSs) in network security?

A) Analyze network traffic for signatures matching known cyberattacks

B) Analyze packets and stop them from being delivered based on detected attacks

C) Translate intent-based configurations into device-specific configurations

D) Provide SSH protocol implementation

155.Which Cisco devices have IPS and firewall capabilities?

A) Cisco ASA 5500-X Series

B) Cisco Catalyst switches

C) Cisco ISR routers

D) Cisco Nexus switches

156.What deployment mode does NOT require an IP address other than for management of Cisco ASA firewalls?

A) Transparent mode

B) Routed mode

C) Hybrid mode

D) Bridge mode

157.What is the purpose of security contexts in Cisco ASA firewalls?

A) To act as standalone virtual firewalls with independent configurations

B) To provide Layer 2 filtering capabilities

C) To enable routing between different VLANs

D) To facilitate VPN connections

158.What is a characteristic of transparent firewalls in Cisco ASA devices?

A) They require IP addresses for inside and outside interfaces

B) They cannot inspect Layer 2 traffic

C) They do not require IP addresses other than for management

D) They are only used for routing purposes

159.Which technology provides detailed analysis and more information than Traditional NetFlow by using deep packet inspection?

A) IPFIX

B) ISAKMP

C) NetFlow

D) Flexible NetFlow

160.What is one of the key advantages of using Flexible NetFlow over Traditional NetFlow?

A) It cannot monitor specific information in packets

B) It is limited to a single flow type

C) It provides user-configurable settings

D) It only supports Layer 3 flows

161.Which protocol provides a packet transport service designed to support several features beyond TCP or UDP capabilities for IPFIX?

A) ICMP

B) SCTP

C) SSH

D) TLS

162.Which open-source tools can be used for analyzing NetFlow?

A) SNMP and NBAR

B) ELK and Graylog

C) SSH and syslog

D) DHCP and DNS

163.What is the primary purpose of NetFlow templates?

A) To export flow information to multiple collectors

B) To provide vendor-neutral support for NetFlow applications

C) To classify most application layer traffic

D) To ensure backward compatibility with NetFlow services

164.Which version of NetFlow is template-based?

A) NetFlow v5

B) NetFlow v7

C) NetFlow v9

D) NetFlow v10

165.What is the recommended duration for capturing NetFlow v9 packets?

A) At least one minute

B) At least three minutes

C) At least five minutes

D) At least ten minutes

166.What is the purpose of IPFIX?

A) To provide vendor-specific NetFlow support

B) To export extracted fields from NBAR

C) To support traditional NetFlow services

D) To serve as an open standard for flow export

167.Which technology extension of NetFlow is sometimes referred to as "NetFlow v10"?

A) SNMP

B) IPFIX

C) SCTP

D) TLS

168.What is the primary benefit of using Flexible NetFlow?

A) It requires fewer resources for data capture

B) It supports only Layer 3 flows

C) It provides detailed analysis using deep packet inspection

D) It is limited to a single flow type

169.Which IOS command is used to configure a NetFlow exporter?

A) ip flow-export version

B) ip flow-export destination

C) ip flow-export template

D) ip flow-export source

170.What is the key advantage of using Flexible NetFlow's immediate and permanent flows?

A) They are easier to configure than normal flows

B) They provide more detailed traffic analysis

C) They have lower overhead for data capture

D) They are limited to Layer 3 traffic

171.Which command is used to verify NetFlow operations and statistics on Cisco IOS devices?

A) show ip flow export

B) show ip flow top-talkers

C) show ip flow cache

D) show ip flow interface

172.Which Cisco devices support Traditional NetFlow (TNF)?

A) Cisco ASA Firewalls

B) Cisco Catalyst switches

C) Cisco ISR routers

D) Cisco Nexus switches

173.Which Cisco devices support Flexible NetFlow (FNF)?

A) Cisco ASA Firewalls

B) Cisco Catalyst switches

C) Cisco ISR routers

D) Cisco Nexus switches

174.What is the primary difference between IPFIX and NetFlow v9?

A) IPFIX is an open standard, while NetFlow v9 is Cisco proprietary

B) IPFIX uses SCTP for packet transport, while NetFlow v9 uses TCP

C) IPFIX supports additional fields from NBAR, while NetFlow v9 does not

D) IPFIX provides backward compatibility with NetFlow v5, while NetFlow v9 does not

175.What is the primary purpose of FlowSets in NetFlow v9?

A) To export flow information to multiple collectors

B) To provide a description of fields present in future data FlowSets

C) To classify application layer traffic

D) To ensure backward compatibility with NetFlow services

176.Which technology allows you to monitor specific information in packets and have different flow types in Flexible NetFlow?

A) SNMP

B) ICMP

C) Deep packet inspection

D) TLS

177.What is the main purpose of Stream Control Transmission Protocol (SCTP) in IPFIX?

A) To provide vendor-specific NetFlow support

B) To support traditional NetFlow services

C) To export extracted fields from NBAR

D) To provide a packet transport service with additional features

178.What command is used to configure NetFlow data exported in Cisco IOS devices?

A) ip flow-export version

B) ip flow-export destination

C) ip flow-export template

D) ip flow-export source

179.What does NetFlow v9 capture that Traditional NetFlow does not?

A) Deep packet inspection information

B) Layer 2 flow information

C) Traffic analysis in separate caches

D) IPv6 flow information

180.Which of the following is a benefit of using NetFlow templates?

A) They provide detailed traffic analysis

B) They allow for future enhancements without fundamental changes

C) They support only Layer 3 flows

D) They export flow information to multiple collectors

181.What is the primary advantage of using IPFIX over NetFlow v9?

A) It supports only Layer 3 flows

B) It provides vendor-specific NetFlow support

C) It is an open standard supported by many networking vendors

D) It captures deep packet inspection information

182.What is the primary purpose of NetFlow templates?

A) To capture traffic analysis in separate caches

B) To provide vendor-specific support for NetFlow applications

C) To support only Layer 3 flows

D) To serve as an open standard for flow export

183.How long is it recommended to capture NetFlow v9 packets to ensure proper decoding?

A) 1 minute

B) 3 minutes

C) At least five minutes

D) Until a template packet is seen

184.Which command is used to configure NetFlow data exported in Cisco IOS devices?

A) ip flow-export version

B) ip flow-export destination

C) ip flow-export template

D) ip flow-export cache

185.What is the key advantage of using Flexible NetFlow's immediate and permanent flows?

A) They provide basic traffic analysis

B) They support only Layer 3 flows

C) They provide more detailed traffic analysis

D) They capture flow information in separate caches

186. Which Cisco resource can you use to learn about network programmability and get some sample codes?

A) ACI

B) DEVNET

C) APIC

D) NETCONF

187. A YANG-based server publishes a set of YANG modules. What will it form if the modules are taken together?

A) NETCONF model

B) RESTCONF model

C) YANG model

D) gRPC model

188.What is the main purpose of Stream Control Transmission Protocol (SCTP) in IPFIX?

A) To provide basic packet transport service

B) To serve as a proprietary protocol for flow export

C) To provide a packet transport service with additional features

D) To support only IPv6 flow information

189.Which command is used to verify NetFlow operations and statistics on Cisco IOS devices?

A) show ip flow cache

B) show ip flow export

C) show ip flow record

D) show ip flow monitor

190. In which type of authentication is a user required to provide a secret that is not known by anyone else?

A) PIN code

B) Authentication by password

C) Authentication by characteristics

D) Authentication by knowledge

191. Which of the following is a set of attributes that can be used if you want to prove a subject's identity only one time?

A) Out-of-band (OOB)

B) One-time passcode (OTP)

C) Biometrics

D) None of the above

192.What are the primary capabilities of Flexible NetFlow?

A) Basic traffic analysis

B) Detailed traffic analysis and deep packet inspection

C) Layer 3 flow analysis only

D) Support for IPv4 flows only

193.What type of flow monitoring does Flexible NetFlow support?

A) Normal, immediate, and permanent

B) Immediate and permanent only

C) Normal and immediate only

D) Normal and permanent only

194.Which feature of Flexible NetFlow allows for monitoring of any specific information in IP traffic?

A) Flow exporters

B) Flow monitors

C) Flow records

D) Flow samplers

195.How can Flexible NetFlow be configured to capture specific types of traffic?

A) By configuring flow samplers

B) By configuring flow exporters with ACLs

C) By configuring flow monitors with ACLs

D) By configuring flow records with ACLs

196.What do Cisco ASA security contexts allow for?

A) Partitioning of the firewall into virtual firewalls

B) Integration with third-party firewalls

C) Unified management of multiple firewalls

D) Enforcement of Layer 3 ACLs

197.What are the deployment modes of Cisco FTD devices?

A) Transparent mode only

B) Routed mode only

C) Routed and inline mode

D) Routed, transparent, and inline mode

198.Which deployment mode of Cisco FTD operates as a next-generation firewall (NGFW) and next-generation intrusion prevention system (NGIPS)?

A) Routed mode

B) Transparent mode

C) Inline mode

D) Virtual mode

199.What is the primary purpose of NetFlow data analysis?

A) To detect Layer 2 attacks

B) To monitor real-time network traffic

C) To identify trends and anomalies in network behavior

D) To configure access control lists (ACLs)

200.What open-source tools can be used for analyzing NetFlow data?

A) SiLK, ELK, and Graylog

B) Cisco Stealthwatch and FlowCollector

C) Cisco NBAR and FlowSensor

D) Cisco Stealthwatch Management Console

201.How can NetFlow templates benefit companies developing NetFlow applications?

A) By providing backward compatibility

B) By avoiding reinvention of products for each new NetFlow feature

C) By supporting only vendor-specific features

D) By offering support for Layer 3 flows only

202.What technology can spread across multiple switches and treat each VLAN as its own subnet or broadcast domain?

A) ARP Spoofing

B) VLANs

C) DHCP Snooping

D) MAC Address Attacks

203.What is the primary benefit of VLANs?

A) Increasing broadcast storm impact

B) Decreasing network performance

C) Reducing broadcast domains

D) Increasing the number of hosts in a domain

204.What is a potential consequence of MAC address flooding attacks?

A) Decreased CPU load on the switch

B) Improved network performance

C) Switch behaving like a hub

D) Enhanced security of the network

205.Which feature is used to prevent MAC address attacks?

A) DHCP Snooping

B) Dynamic ARP Inspection

C) Port Security

D) VLAN Trunking Protocol (VTP)

206. What is the purpose of DHCP Rogue Attack?

A) To assign IP addresses to authorized devices

B) To deny service to authorized users

C) To redirect traffic to a fake gateway

D) To intercept sensitive data from the network

207.Which security feature protects networks against Man-in-the-Middle ARP spoofing attacks?

A) DHCP Snooping

B) Port Security

C) Dynamic ARP Inspection

D) Control Plane Policing

208.What is ARP Spoofing?

A) A form of DDoS attack

B) A method to alter IP packet paths

C) A type of VLAN configuration

D) A form of Man-in-the-Middle attack

209.Which plane of a network device is responsible for forwarding data?

A) Management plane

B) Control plane

C) Data plane

D) Security plane

210.What is the purpose of Control Plane Policing (CoPP)?

A) To manage traffic flow of control plane packets

B) To protect the data plane from attacks

C) To configure QoS on the management plane

D) To prevent broadcast storms

211.What is the primary function of IP options?

A) To improve network performance

B) To alter the path of packets

C) To reduce CPU load on devices

D) To increase security of the network

212.Which command disables the transmission of ICMP redirects?

A) ip options drop

B) no ip redirects

C) ip source-route

D) ip verify

213.What feature can be used to verify the source address of a forwarded packet?

A) DHCP Snooping

B) Unicast RPF

C) Port Security

D) MAC Address Filtering

214.Which mode of Unicast RPF is preferred in cases of asymmetric routing?

A) Loose mode

B) Strict mode

C) Dynamic mode

D) Aggressive mode

215.What does the Management Plane Protection (MPP) feature restrict?

A) Data plane traffic

B) Control plane traffic

C) Management plane traffic

D) VLAN traffic

216.How does VLANs reduce security risks?

A) By increasing broadcast domains

B) By increasing the number of hosts receiving frames

C) By reducing the number of hosts receiving frames

D) By reducing network performance

217.Which attack involves flooding a switch with fake MAC addresses?

A) DHCP Rogue Attack

B) ARP Spoofing

C) MAC Address Flooding Attack

D) Dynamic ARP Inspection

218.Which security feature prevents a network attacker from sending large numbers of Ethernet frames with forged source MAC addresses?

A) DHCP Snooping

B) Dynamic ARP Inspection

C) Port Security

D) VLAN Trunking Protocol (VTP)

219. Which of the following open source projects are used in various single sign-on implementations and mainly for exchanging authorization and authentication data between the two peers (identity providers)?

A) OAuth 2.0

B) DUO security

C) SAML

D) OpenConnectID

220.What does Dynamic ARP Inspection (DAI) protect against?

A) ARP Spoofing

B) MAC Address Flooding Attack

C) DHCP Rogue Attack

D) VLAN Hopping

221. What is the purpose of a CI/CD pipeline?

A) To manage cloud resources

B) To develop, test, and deploy code rapidly and reliably

C) To secure cloud applications

D) To increase storage capacity

222.What does the term "scalability" refer to in cloud computing?

A) Increasing network bandwidth

B) The ability to increase or decrease resources as needed

C) Enhancing security features

D) Reducing operational costs

223.How does Cisco define DevSecOps?

A) The integration of development, security, and operations

B) The separation of development and operations

C) The enhancement of security operations only

D) The optimization of development processes only

224.What is the primary function of an IaaS model in cloud computing?

A) Providing software applications to end-users

B) Offering on-demand access to physical and virtual infrastructure resources

C) Delivering a platform for developing, running, and managing applications

D) Securing cloud resources

225. Which of the following defines permissions and access rights to someone?

A) An accounting model

B) An authorization model

C) A mandatory access control model
D) An authentication model

226.Which cloud model is typically used by multiple organizations with similar goals and requirements?

A) Public Cloud

B) Private Cloud

C) Hybrid Cloud

D) Community Cloud

227.How does a cloud access security broker (CASB) like Cisco Cloudlock enhance cloud security?

A) By providing additional data storage

B) By optimizing network performance

C) By offering tools to secure cloud applications and data

D) By managing development tools

228.What is the role of Cisco Secure Workload in cloud environments?

A) To manage cloud resources

B) To enhance application security and compliance

C) To provide cloud storage

D) To optimize network performance

229.What is a key advantage of using containers in cloud computing?

A) Improved physical security

B) Enhanced network performance

C) Increased storage capacity

D) Efficient application deployment and scaling

230Which type of cloud deployment model combines both private and public clouds?

A) Public Cloud

B) Private Cloud

C) Hybrid Cloud

D) Community Cloud

231.What is one of the main features of the IaaS model in cloud computing?

A) It provides application development frameworks.

B) It offers managed software applications.

C) It delivers virtualized computing resources over the internet.

D) It allows for the deployment of web applications.

232.What is the primary focus of Cisco Cloudlock?

A) Cloud data storage

B) Network optimization

C) Cloud security and compliance

D) Application development

233. Which of the following standards can a network access device (switch or wireless access point) use to enable port-based access control, i.e., allows traffic to access the port only after authorization and authentication?

A) 802.1Q

B) 802.11ac

C) pxGrid

D) 802.1X

234.What does the term "elasticity" refer to in cloud computing?

A) The ability to store large amounts of data

B) The ability to automatically increase or decrease IT resources as needed

C) The ability to secure data in the cloud

D) The ability to develop and deploy applications

235.What does the Cisco Secure Workload product focus on?

A) Providing additional data storage

B) Enhancing security for cloud-native applications

C) Improving network performance

D) Offering application development tools

236.In which cloud service model does the provider manage the operating system, but the customer manages the application and data?

A) SaaS

B) PaaS

C) IaaS

D) DaaS

237.What is the main advantage of cloud-native applications?

A) They require no internet connection

B) They are optimized for cloud environments, allowing for better scalability and performance

C) They are developed using traditional IT infrastructure

D) They are primarily used in on-premises data centers

238.What is a CASB and how does it enhance cloud security?

A) A Cloud Application Security Broker that provides data storage

B) A Cloud Access Security Broker that monitors and secures cloud applications

C) A Cloud Access Service Builder that optimizes network performance

D) A Cloud Application Service Builder that enhances application development

239.Which cloud model provides the highest level of physical control over the infrastructure?

A) Public Cloud

B) Private Cloud

C) Hybrid Cloud

D) Community Cloud

240. What is the primary benefit of using PaaS for developers?

A) Full control over physical infrastructure

B) Simplified deployment and management of applications

C) Enhanced network performance

D) Increased data storage capacity

241.How does Cisco define "cloud-native" applications?

A) Applications that can only be run on private cloud infrastructure

B) Applications specifically designed to take advantage of cloud computing models

C) Applications developed for traditional on-premises data centers

D) Applications that do not require cloud services

242.Which cloud service model is ideal for organizations that need to run their own applications but do not want to manage the underlying hardware?

A) SaaS

B) PaaS

C) IaaS

D) DaaS

243.What does the term "orchestration" refer to in the context of containerized applications?

A) Manual deployment of applications

B) Automated deployment, scaling, and management of containerized applications

C) Development of software applications

D) Securing cloud environments

244.What is the primary function of a cloud logging solution?

A) Improving data storage capacity

B) Enhancing network performance

C) Monitoring and analyzing security events and compliance

D) Reducing cloud service costs

245. Which cloud service model offers the highest level of abstraction from the underlying hardware for end-users?

A) SaaS

B) PaaS

C) IaaS

D) DaaS

246.What is the primary role of Cisco Secure Workload in securing cloud environments?

A) Data encryption

B) Application development

C) Enhancing security and compliance through visibility and segmentation

D) Network optimization

247.What does the acronym CI/CD stand for?

A) Continuous Integration/Continuous Deployment

B) Cloud Integration/Cloud Deployment

C) Continuous Improvement/Continuous Development

D) Cloud Infrastructure/Cloud Development

248. Which cloud model involves resources dedicated to a single organization but can be hosted by a third-party provider?

A) Public Cloud

B) Private Cloud

C) Hybrid Cloud

D) Community Cloud

249. How does a hybrid cloud model benefit an organization?

A) It offers unlimited storage capacity

B) It combines the scalability of public cloud with the security of private cloud

C) It eliminates the need for an on-premises data center

D) It reduces the need for cloud security measures

250.What is the purpose of a cloud security assessment?

A) To increase network speed

B) To evaluate and enhance the security posture of cloud infrastructure

C) To improve data storage efficiency

D) To develop cloud-native applications

251. Which cloud model is ideal for organizations with highly sensitive data and stringent security requirements?

A) Public Cloud

B) Private Cloud

C) Hybrid Cloud

D) Community Cloud

252.What does Cisco recommend for ensuring secure access to cloud services?

A) Using a single sign-on (SSO) solution

B) Encrypting data at rest

C) Implementing a Cloud Access Security Broker (CASB)

D) Increasing network bandwidth

253.What is the primary advantage of using containers for application deployment?

A) Improved physical security

B) Increased data storage

C) Enhanced scalability and portability of applications

D) Reduced cost of cloud services

254.In the context of cloud computing, what is "multi-tenancy"?

A) Multiple users sharing a single cloud resource

B) A single user accessing multiple cloud resources

C) Multiple cloud providers offering the same service

D) A single user with multiple accounts

255.What is the main function of Cisco Cloudlock in a cloud environment?

A) To enhance cloud storage capabilities

B) To optimize network performance

C) To provide cloud security and compliance management

D) To offer development tools for cloud applications

256.What is a significant benefit of using a SaaS model?

A) Control over the underlying hardware

B) Simplified software deployment and maintenance

C) Increased physical security

D) Enhanced application development capabilities

257.Which cloud model allows an organization to maintain control over sensitive data

while leveraging public cloud resources for scalability?

A) Public Cloud

B) Private Cloud

C) Hybrid Cloud

D) Community Cloud

258.What is one of the primary functions of Cisco Secure Workload?

A) To manage data storage

B) To optimize network traffic

C) To provide security and visibility for cloud-native applications

D) To enhance application development

259.What determines the action taken by ACP rules in Cisco FMC?

A) Source IP only

B) Destination IP only

C) Application only

D) Contextual information including application, user, URL, payload, etc.

260.What is a key point about URL filtering in Firepower Management Center?

A) It uses URL lists for filtering

B) It disregards subdomains within subject common names

C) It only matches HTTP traffic

D) It doesn't evaluate the reputation of URLs

261.What feature of the Firepower system requires additional licensing for protecting against malicious software?

A) URL filtering

B) Access control policies

C) Intrusion policies

D) Malware protection

262.Which technology provides network visibility throughout the full attack continuum?

A) Cisco ISE

B) NetFlow

C) IPFIX

D) Intrusion Prevention System (IPS)

263.How many security models does SNMPv3 provide?

A) One

B) Two

C) Three

D) Four

264.What is the primary objective of access controls?

A) To enhance network performance

B) To protect information from unauthorized access

C) To reduce network segmentation

D) To increase network traffic

265.Which command activates AAA features on Cisco devices?

A) aaa new-model

B) aaa authentication login

C) aaa group server

D) aaa authorization exec

266.What does DAC stand for in access control mechanisms?

A) Data Access Control

B) Discretionary Access Control

C) Dynamic Access Control

D) Device Access Control

267.How many phases does ISAKMP negotiation consist of?

A) One

B) Two

C) Three

D) Four

268.What does IPsec provide for the transmission of sensitive information over unprotected networks?

A) Encryption only

B) Authentication only

C) Both encryption and authentication

D) Compression only

269.What is the primary function of the Cisco AnyConnect client?

A) VPN termination

B) Network routing

C) Network monitoring

D) Network optimization

270.Which command is used to upload the AnyConnect image to a router's flash memory?

A) upload anyconnect

B) copy tftp flash

C) install anyconnect

D) configure anyconnect

271.How are RSA keys generated on a Cisco router?

A) Using the crypto generate rsa command

B) Using the ssh generate key command

C) Using the rsa generate key command

D) Using the key generate rsa command

272.Which command is used to create a trustpoint on a Cisco router?

A) crypto pki trustpoint

B) trustpoint create

C) trustpoint crypto

D) pki trustpoint create

273.What is the purpose of a trustpoint in VPN configuration?

A) To authenticate users

B) To configure encryption algorithms

C) To establish secure communication

D) To manage VPN policies

274.What protocol does NTP use for time synchronization?

A) TCP

B) UDP

C) HTTP

D) ICMP

275.Which SNMP version provides secure access to devices by encrypting and authenticating data packets?

A) SNMPv1

B) SNMPv2c

C) SNMPv3

D) SNMPv4

276.Which security features are provided by SNMPv3?

A) Message integrity and authentication

B) Authentication and encryption

C) Message integrity and encryption

D) Authentication, encryption, and message integrity

277.What is the purpose of ACLs in VPN configuration?

A) To control access to network resources

B) To establish VPN tunnels

C) To authenticate VPN users

D) To encrypt VPN traffic

278.What is the significance of configuring NAT in VPN tunnels?

A) To encrypt traffic

B) To increase network performance

C) To allow access to public resources

D) To prevent NAT traversal issues

279.What is the primary function of site-to-site IPsec VPN tunnels?

A) To provide secure remote access for users

B) To connect multiple branch offices securely

C) To monitor network traffic

D) To optimize network performance

280.How are IPsec VPN tunnels encrypted and authenticated?

A) Using TLS

B) Using ISAKMP and ESP

C) Using HTTP

D) Using UDP

281.What is the primary purpose of NTP authentication?

A) To synchronize time across devices

B) To ensure the accuracy of timestamps

C) To encrypt NTP packets

D) To verify the authenticity of NTP servers

282. What is the primary function of a web proxy server?

A) Enhance web performance

B) Protect end users from connecting to malicious websites

C) Reduce bandwidth usage

D) Improve server uptime

283. Which logging protocol is recommended for real-time visibility into logs?

A) UDP

B) HTTP

C) TCP

D) RELP

284. What is the benefit of centralized logging?

A) Reduced storage costs

B) Simplified log format

C) Correlating logs from different infrastructures and application sources

D) Increased data privacy

285.What does log replication involve?

A) Writing logs to a local disk

B) Transporting logs using an API

C) Setting up a cron job to replicate log files on a Linux server to a central server

D) Using UDP to transmit logs

286.What are the core components of any security program related to logs?

A) Log analysis and storage

B) Log replication, transport, and collection

C) Log retention and deletion

D) Log encryption and decryption

287.What should be the main consideration when configuring log storage?

A) Log format

B) Network bandwidth

C) Storage scalability and log retention period

D) Type of operating system

288.How does a web proxy improve user privacy?

A) By blocking all user connections

B) By hiding the user's IP address

C) By encrypting web requests

D) By storing all user data

289. What is the primary function of a web proxy server?

A) To block access to websites based on user preferences

B) To improve security and privacy

C) To manage network bandwidth efficiently

D) To encrypt all incoming and outgoing web traffic

290.What is the function of URL filtering in a web proxy?

A) Logging all web requests

B) Caching web content

C) Blocking access to non-conformant websites

D) Reducing bandwidth usage

291.Which of the following describes application whitelisting?

A) Blocking a list of suspicious or malicious sites

B) Allowing access required for the application to function while blocking everything else

C) Encrypting all application data

D) Monitoring and logging application activity

292.What type of policy does a traditional security policy implement?

A) Allow-list policy

B) Whitelist policy

C) Block-list policy

D) Zero trust policy

293.How can a baseline of normal activity in an application be established?

A) By scanning for vulnerabilities

B) By monitoring application behavior over time

C) By implementing a block-list policy

D) By storing logs on local disks

294.What is the role of the application server in the sample distributed application?

A) Service user requests

B) Process business logic

C) Store data

D) Monitor network traffic

295. Which ports are typically associated with the web server in the sample distributed application?

A) 80 and 443

B) 3306 and 1433

C) 22 and 21

D) 25 and 110

296.What is the benefit of defining logging levels?

A) Increased log volume

B) Improved log encryption

C) Filtering and extracting useful information

D) Reduced storage scalability

297.How can network services dependencies be identified in a large distributed application environment?

A) Using documentation and operating system tools like netstat and lsof

B) Implementing a block-list policy

C) Encrypting all network traffic

D) Disabling unused network services

298.What should be considered when configuring the storage method for logs?

A) Type of operating system

B) Application verbosity and storage requirements

C) Network bandwidth

D) Encryption level

299.What type of connection protocol is recommended for transmitting logs to ensure reliability?

A) UDP

B) HTTP

C) TCP

D) FTP

300.Why is it important to have a centralized logging system?

A) To reduce network traffic

B) To correlate logs from various sources for a holistic view

C) To simplify log format

D) To increase data encryption

301. How can vulnerabilities in installed software be detected?

A) By setting up a cron job

B) By using vulnerability analysis comparing files against known vulnerabilities

C) By implementing an allow-list policy

D) By monitoring application behavior

302.What does RELP stand for?

A) Reliable Event Logging Protocol

B) Real-time Event Logging Protocol

C) Remote Event Logging Protocol

D) Redundant Event Logging Protocol

303.What is the primary goal of log analysis?

A) To define baselines and understand patterns and anomalies

B) To increase storage capacity

C) To simplify log formats

D) To reduce network traffic

304.What is an important aspect of application security solutions regarding infrastructure independence?

A) They should work only on virtual machines

B) They should not depend on the application hosting infrastructure

C) They should only support public cloud environments

D) They should be based on the operating system used

305.What is a key function of Cisco Secure Web Appliance's web reputation engine?

A) Blocking all web traffic

B) Categorizing attributes to determine website risk

C) Improving web performance

D) Reducing outgoing bandwidth

306.How does centralized logging help with compliance requirements?

A) By reducing log volume

B) By ensuring all web activity is logged

C) By encrypting logs

D) By standardizing log formats

307.What is the function of netstat and lsof tools in application security?

A) Encrypting network traffic

B) Monitoring network services and identifying dependencies

C) Logging user activity

D) Implementing an allow-list policy

308.What is a key benefit of using Transmission Control Protocol (TCP) for log transmission?

A) Lower bandwidth usage

B) Reliability and data integrity

C) Faster transmission speeds

D) Simpler implementation

309.What should be done to logs on local disks by default?

A) They should be encrypted

B) They should be compressed

C) They should be written to files

D) They should be deleted regularly

310.What does WCCP stand for?

A) Web Cache Communication Protocol

B) Web Content Communication Protocol

C) Web Cache Control Protocol

D) Web Content Control Protocol

311.Which network protocol is generally less reliable for log transmission?

A) TCP

B) UDP

C) RELP

D) HTTP

312.What is the advantage of proxy cache in a Cisco Secure Web Appliance?

A) Improved web performance and reduced outgoing bandwidth

B) Enhanced data encryption

C) Simplified user management

D) Increased log volume

313.Why is it important to configure applications to write log events directly to a centralized log management system?

A) To reduce disk usage

B) To enable real-time visibility and monitoring

C) To simplify log format

D) To encrypt logs

314.What type of policy blocks everything by default and explicitly allows required access?

A) Block-list policy

B) Allow-list policy

C) Zero trust policy

D) Encryption policy

315.What is a primary function of a web proxy server in terms of performance?

A) Encrypting all web traffic

B) Caching content from popular websites

C) Blocking malicious websites

D) Logging all web requests

316.How does the Cisco Secure Web Appliance protect user privacy?

A) By hiding the end user's IP address

B) By encrypting web traffic

C) By logging all web activity

D) By blocking non-conformant websites

317. What should be done to reduce information overload and disk storage consumption in logging?

A) Increase log retention period

B) Define specific logging levels

C) Use UDP for log transmission

D) Encrypt all logs

318.What should the centralized logging system provide for effective log analysis?

A) Higher bandwidth

B) Real-time data visualization tools

C) Simplified log formats

D) Encrypted log storage

319.What is the role of an application server in a distributed application?

A) Servicing user requests

B) Processing business logic

C) Storing data

D) Monitoring network traffic

320.Which technology helps to establish a baseline of normal application activity?

A) Vulnerability scanning

B) Behavior monitoring over time

C) Block-list policies

D) Application whitelisting

321.What type of logs should be stored in a centralized repository?

A) Only critical logs

B) All logs including applications, networking devices, workstations, and servers

C) Only security-related logs

D) Logs from servers only

322. What does TLS stand for?

A) Transmission Layer Security

B) Transport Layer Security

C) Transaction Layer Security

D) Transfer Layer Security

323.Which method is not recommended for log transportation?

A) API

B) TCP

C) RELP

D) UDP

324.What is the primary advantage of centralized logging?

A) Simplified log format

B) Correlation of logs for a holistic view

C) Reduced log volume

D) Increased storage capacity

325.Which feature of the Cisco Secure Web Appliance categorizes attributes to determine website risk?

A) Proxy cache

B) Web reputation engine

C) URL filtering

D) Web traffic logging

326.What should be considered when defining the log retention period?

A) Type of operating system

B) Type of applications and their logging verbosity

C) Network bandwidth

D) User privacy policies

327.How can you improve web performance using a proxy server?

A) By encrypting all web traffic

B) By caching content from popular websites

C) By logging all web requests

D) By blocking all non-conformant websites

328.Why is it important to use a reliable protocol like RELP or TCP for log transmission?

A) To ensure data integrity and reliability

B) To reduce bandwidth usage

C) To simplify log format

D) To increase transmission speed

329.How does a web proxy control internet access?

A) By logging all web requests

B) By encrypting web traffic

C) By blocking access to websites not in conformance with the acceptable use policy

D) By caching web content

330.What is the purpose of using a web proxy server's PAC file?

A) To configure automatic proxy settings for the client

B) To log all web activity

C) To encrypt user data

D) To block non-conformant websites

331. What is the new name for AMP for Endpoints?

A) Cisco Secure Malware

B) Cisco Endpoint Protection

C) Cisco Secure Endpoint

D) Cisco Threat Analytics

332.What is the primary focus of Endpoint Detection and Response (EDR)?

A) Data encryption

B) Detecting and investigating suspicious activities on endpoints

C) Network monitoring

D) Patch management

333.Which of the following is NOT a key aspect of an effective EDR solution?

A) Filtering

B) Threat blocking

C) Assisting with digital forensics and incident response

D) Data encryption

334.What term is used to describe security solutions that address endpoint security and protect against exploits and attacks?

A) Endpoint detection and response (EDR)

B) Endpoint protection (EPP)

C) Mobile device management (MDM)

D) Multifactor authentication (MFA)

335.Where is the majority of data processing performed for Cisco Secure Endpoint?

A) On the endpoint device

B) In the cloud

C) On a local server

D) In the data center

336.What feature of Cisco Secure Endpoint leverages cloud-delivered intelligence to monitor files, scripts, and network activity?

A) Classic signature-based protection

B) Exploit prevention

C) Device flow correlation

D) Dynamic file analysis

337.What is the purpose of retrospective security in Cisco Secure Endpoint?

A) To block files using SHA-256 hashes or signatures

B) To monitor and analyze files for changing threat levels

C) To provide offline malware detection

D) To create allow and block lists

338.What capability allows Cisco Secure Endpoint to block families of malware that rely on polymorphism?

A) One-to-one file protection

B) Fuzzy fingerprinting

C) Machine learning models

D) Device flow correlation

339.What type of indicators of compromise help surface suspicious activity observed on the endpoints through cloud-based pattern recognition?

A) Endpoint IoCs

B) Antivirus IoCs

C) Cloud IoCs

D) Custom IoCs

340.What type of analysis can correlate samples with millions of other samples and billions of artifacts in Cisco Secure Endpoint?

A) Static file analysis

B) Dynamic file analysis

C) Retrospective analysis

D) Behavioral analysis

341.What are custom detections in Cisco Secure Endpoint used for?

A) Creating application allow and block lists

B) Generating prevent lists

C) Analyzing network traffic

D) Correlating malware samples

342.What feature in Cisco Secure Endpoint stops the execution of programs on hosts but does not quarantine them?

A) Custom detections

B) Blocked Applications

C) Allowed Applications

D) Retrospective security

343.What type of exclusion set excludes files or paths using wildcards for filenames, extensions, or paths?

A) Threat exclusion

B) Extension exclusion

C) Wildcard exclusion

D) Path exclusion

344.What is required to make edits to an uploaded IP list in Cisco Secure Endpoint?

A) Directly editing the file in the console

B) Downloading, editing, and re-uploading the file

C) Using the cloud-based editing tool

D) Submitting a request to Cisco support

345.What does the Blocked Applications feature do?

A) Quarantines suspicious files

B) Stops the execution of programs on hosts

C) Deletes malicious applications

D) Prevents the installation of new software

346.What type of custom exclusion set can be updated by Cisco and pushed to endpoints?

A) Cisco-maintained exclusions

B) Organization-maintained exclusions

C) User-defined exclusions

D) Automated exclusions

347.Which of the following is NOT a reason for employing endpoint security?

A) To maintain visibility and enforce policy during an attack

B) To ensure compliance with decryption policies

C) To protect offline users from threats

D) To prevent all internet traffic

348.How does Cisco Secure Endpoint ensure that custom-built applications do not get quarantined?

A) By using antivirus software

B) By creating allow lists

C) By using fuzzy fingerprinting

D) By performing retrospective analysis

349.What type of engine provides on-disk malware detection in Cisco Secure Endpoint?

A) Behavioral analysis engine

B) Machine learning engine

C) Signature-based engine

D) Heuristic analysis engine

350.What are endpoint indicators of compromise (IoCs) used for in Cisco Secure Endpoint?

A) Blocking IP communications

B) Creating custom detection lists

C) Scanning post-compromise indicators across multiple endpoints

D) Providing offline malware detection

351.What type of file analysis provides a video of file detonation and an analysis report in Cisco Secure Endpoint?

A) Static file analysis

B) Dynamic file analysis

C) Retrospective analysis

D) Behavioral analysis

352.What can organizations use to supplement Cisco's threat intelligence in Secure Endpoint?

A) Custom exclusions

B) Block lists and allow lists

C) Static and dynamic analysis

D) Machine learning models

353.What is the benefit of cloud-based malware detection in Cisco Secure Endpoint?

A) Faster processing on the endpoint

B) Reduced need for regular updates

C) Rapid updates leveraging cloud resources

D) Complete offline functionality

354.What does the Endpoint Indicators of Compromise (IoCs) feature provide?

A) A list of blocked applications

B) A powerful threat-hunting capability

C) On-disk malware detection

D) Exploit prevention

355.How can organizations manage the exclusion of specific detections by threat name?

A) By using the Threat exclusion set

B) By creating custom detection lists

C) By leveraging the Cisco-maintained exclusions

D) By using retrospective security

356.Which component of Cisco Secure Endpoint can block malicious IP communications to and from the endpoint?

a) Fuzzy fingerprinting

b) Device flow correlation

c) Machine learning models

d) Exploit prevention

357.How can an organization prevent the execution of programs that are critical but vulnerable?

A) By quarantining the program

B) By blocking the program

C) By creating an exclusion set

D) By using retrospective security

358.What type of policy component can be used to resolve conflicts with other security products?

A) Custom detections

B) Application control

C) Exclusion sets

D) Endpoint IoCs

359.What is required to create and name a list of allowed or blocked applications in Cisco Secure Endpoint?

A) Uploading the application

B) Entering the SHA-256 hash

C) Both A and B

D) Editing the application code

360.What does dynamic file analysis in Cisco Secure Endpoint leverage?

A) Static attributes

B) Behavioral indicators

C) Retrospective security

D) Cloud-based pattern recognition

361.How are updates to Cisco-maintained exclusions pushed to endpoints?

A) Through manual updates

B) Automatically by policy

C) Via endpoint user action

D) By downloading from the console

362.What type of custom detection list can be created to manage applications in Cisco Secure Endpoint?

A) Application control list

B) Endpoint IoCs

C) Network control list

D) Threat exclusion list

363.Why is endpoint security essential for users who access the Internet while offline?

A) To maintain network performance

B) To provide patch management

C) To protect against threats like malware and ransomware

D) To enforce corporate policy

364.How are large file or database performance issues mitigated in Cisco Secure Endpoint?

A) By using machine learning models

B) By creating exclusion sets

C) By applying threat blocking

D) By performing dynamic file analysis

365.What allows Secure Endpoint to remain lightweight while performing various functions?

A) On-premises data processing

B) Cloud-based detection and analysis

C) Endpoint-based signature updates

D) Offline detection engine

366.Which feature in Cisco Secure Endpoint helps with proactive threat hunting?

A) Retrospective security

B) Endpoint IoCs

C) Custom detections

D) Dynamic file analysis

367.How are changes to IP lists logged in Cisco Secure Endpoint?

A) Automatically in the cloud

B) Through manual entry

C) In an audit log

D) By endpoint user action

368.What is the benefit of using custom detections in Secure Endpoint?

A) To perform offline malware detection

B) To provide retrospective analysis

C) To create specific prevent lists

D) To monitor network activity

369.What allows Secure Endpoint to perform in-memory attack prevention?

A) Classic signature-based protection

B) Exploit prevention

C) Device flow correlation

D) Retrospective security

370.Which component helps to block files based on SHA-256 hashes or signatures?

A) One-to-one file protection

B) Fuzzy fingerprinting

C) Machine learning models

D) Endpoint IoCs

371.What is an essential term used to describe the management of mobile devices within an organization?

A) EPP

B) EDR

C) MDM

D) MFA

372.What does Cisco Secure Endpoint use to identify malicious files based on static attributes?

A) Behavioral analysis

B) Machine learning models

C) Fuzzy fingerprinting

D) Retrospective security

373.What type of IoCs provides a powerful threat-hunting capability for scanning post-compromise indicators across multiple endpoints?

A) Cloud IoCs

B) Custom IoCs

C) Endpoint IoCs

D) Antivirus IoCs

374.What type of exclusion set excludes files with a specific extension?

A) Threat exclusion

B) Extension exclusion

C) Wildcard exclusion

D) Path exclusion

375.Which of the following is NOT included in Cisco Secure Endpoint's detection and protection features?

A) Anti-malware

B) Indicators of compromise

C) Dynamic file analysis

D) Data encryption

376.How does Cisco Secure Endpoint help with digital forensics and incident response (DFIR)?

A) By blocking IP communications

B) By providing retrospective security

C) By assisting with threat response and proactive threat hunting

D) By using fuzzy fingerprinting

377.What is the role of multifactor authentication (MFA) in endpoint security?

A) To detect malware

B) To monitor network activity

C) To ensure secure access

D) To perform patch management

378.How are applications blocked from executing on endpoints using Cisco Secure Endpoint?

A) By creating block lists

B) By using retrospective security

C) By leveraging cloud IoCs

D) By using exploit prevention

379.Which feature in Cisco Secure Endpoint can prevent in-memory attacks on running processes?

A) One-to-one file protection

B) Exploit prevention

C) Fuzzy fingerprinting

D) Device flow correlation

380.What is required for the cloud-based pattern recognition to trigger more in-depth investigations in Cisco Secure Endpoint?

A) Endpoint indicators of compromise (IoCs)

B) Custom detections

C) Network control lists

D) Threat exclusions

381. What is a key benefit of having full lifecycle asset management in an organization?

A) Minimizes employee turnover

B) Establishes a chain of custody for assets

C) Increases software costs

D) Decreases network speed

382. What is one of the most common areas for asset risk mentioned in the text?

A) Server failures

B) Loss or theft of mobile devices

C) Software bugs

D) Network downtimes

383.Which tool provides device management functionality to ensure consistent security across a variety of devices?

A) Cisco WebEx

B) Cisco Meraki Systems Manager

C) Cisco Talos

D) Cisco Firepower

384.What functionality does Cisco Meraki SM include to tag devices and enforce policies?

A) Threat exclusion

B) Sentry functionality

C) Antivirus scanning

D) Firewall management

385.Which type of attack involves an attacker actively trying to log in to applications using many different combinations of credentials?

A) Phishing attack

B) Directory harvest attack

C) Online brute-force attack

D) Man-in-the-middle attack

386.Which type of attack is difficult to detect but requires a great deal of computational resources from the attacker?

A) Online brute-force attack

B) Offline brute-force attack

C) Phishing attack

D) Man-in-the-middle attack

387.What does multifactor authentication (MFA) require beyond just a password?

A) A username

B) A second source of identity validation

C) Biometric data

D) Security questions

388.What is the common term for a single-authentication approach based on a password?

A) Something you have

B) Something you know

C) Something you are

D) Something you do

389.What is a common form of the second source of identity validation in MFA?

A) A software token

B) An email confirmation

C) A CAPTCHA test

D) A security question

390.What type of attack involves an attacker intercepting communication between two sources and impersonating both parties?

A) Directory harvest attack

B) Man-in-the-middle attack

C) Phishing attack

D) Brute-force attack

391.What is a key recommendation to prevent ransomware exposure mentioned in the text?

A) Use single-factor authentication

B) Keep backups online

C) Utilize multifactor authentication

D) Ignore incident response plans

392.What do posture assessments typically include to minimize risk?

A) Network speed tests

B) Social engineering checks

C) Operating system patch checks

D) User satisfaction surveys

393.What capability do MDM tools often provide to administrators for lost or stolen devices?

A) Increase battery life

B) Remotely wipe data or lock the device

C) Install new hardware

D) Disable internet access

394.What does Cisco Meraki SM's sentry functionality NOT use to tag devices and enforce policies?

A) Device type

B) Enrollment type

C) Application version

D) Active Directory group membership

395.Which of the following is NOT a common variable for password strength?

A) Length

B) Complexity

C) Frequency of use

D) Time of day

396.What type of tool provides visibility and security across a variety of mobile devices?

A) Mobile device management (MDM)

B) Network monitoring

C) Endpoint detection

D) Intrusion prevention system

397.What is a common goal of phishing campaigns targeting users?

A) To increase network speed

B) To reduce server load

C) To create business email compromise (BEC)

D) To update user software

398.What is the primary function of multifactor authentication (MFA)?

A) To allow guest access

B) To provide two sources of identity validation

C) To reduce server costs

D) To increase internet speed

399.Which recommendation is NOT provided by the United States Federal Bureau of Investigation's Internet Crime Complaint Center (IC3) to prevent ransomware exposure?

A) Back up data and keep backups offline

B) Utilize multifactor authentication

C) Update and patch systems

D) Increased internet bandwidth

400.What does full lifecycle asset management help organizations track?

A) Software versions

B) Chain of custody for assets

C) Network performance

D) User satisfaction

401.Which type of attack attempts to determine an organization's naming convention to use common passwords?

A) Brute-force attack

B) Phishing attack

C) Directory harvest attack

D) Man-in-the-middle attack

402.What should organizations do to ensure that devices can be updated and patched regardless of their connection to the network?

A) Use a local update server

B) Adopt a cloud approach

C) Disable internet access

D) Use outdated software

403.What is the purpose of endpoint posture assessments?

A) To increase employee productivity

B) To check the patching of operating systems and security software

C) To monitor network speed

D) To reduce server load

404.How can MDM tools help when a device is lost or stolen?

A) Increase internet speed

B) Remotely wipe data or lock the device

C) Update the operating system

D) Disable the device permanently

405.What is a major reason passwords are considered an ineffective approach to authentication?

A) They are too long

B) They are too complex

C) Once known, they are no longer useful

D) They are easy to remember

406.What is one benefit of cloud-based device management?

A) Increased manual updates

B) Consistent security across devices

C) Reduced need for security

D) Higher costs

407.Which attack involves using a fake website to capture a user's login credentials?

A) Brute-force attack

B) Man-in-the-middle attack

C) Directory harvest attack

D) Phishing attack

408. What is a primary function of Cisco Meraki Systems Manager?

A) Antivirus scanning

B) Device management

C) Network routing

D) Software development

409.What does MFA add to the authentication process besides a password?

A) An additional user account

B) Biometric data

C) A second source of identity validation

D) A security question

410.What is an example of "something you have" in the context of MFA?

A) A password

B) A username

C) A physical token

D) A security question

411.What should organizations do when new devices are made available to users?

A) Ignore them

B) Grant immediate access

C) Track and manage them

D) Disable internet access

412.What type of management includes the chain of custody for assets from onboarding to retirement?

A) Software management

B) Network management

C) Full lifecycle asset management

D) User management

413.What is often required for password cracking in offline brute-force attacks?

A) Minimal computational resources

B) Reconnaissance

C) Spoofed environment

D) Encrypted or hashed passwords

414. Which of the following is the entity in charge of transmitting emails from a sender to a recipient, sometimes referred to as the "mail-server"?

A) Mail transfer agent (MTA)

B) Mail delivery agent (MDA)

C) Mail submission agent (MSA)
D) Mail user agent (MUA)

415.What is one key function of Cisco Meraki SM's sentry functionality?

A) Antivirus scanning

B) Tagging devices to enforce policies

C) Increasing network speed

D) Reducing server load

416.What is a benefit of using MDM tools for mobile devices?

A) Increased battery life

B) Consistent security policies

C) Manual software updates

D) Lower costs

417.What does MFA help prevent?

A) High server load

B) Credential brute-force attacks

C) Increased internet speed

D) Reduced software costs

418.What is the primary purpose of a password in authentication?

A) To increase security costs

B) To provide identity validation

C) To reduce internet speed

D) To update software

419.What do endpoint posture assessments typically check?

A) Network speed

B) User satisfaction

C) Patching of operating systems

D) Social engineering techniques

420.What is the common term for a second source of identity validation in MFA?

A) Something you know

B) Something you have

C) Something you are

D) Something you do

421.What is a key recommendation from the IC3 to prevent ransomware exposure?

A) Disable antivirus software

B) Keep backups offline

C) Use simple passwords

D) Ignore incident response plans

422.What does a well-defined patch strategy help prevent?

A) Increased internet speed

B) Higher software costs

C) Exploits and eavesdropping attacks

D) User dissatisfaction

423.What type of attack involves the attacker impersonating both parties in a communication?

A) Phishing attack

B) Directory harvest attack

C) Man-in-the-middle attack

D) Brute-force attack

424.What is a primary benefit of multifactor authentication (MFA)?

A) Reduced need for user accounts

B) Increased manual updates

C) Enhanced security through additional identity validation

D) Lower costs

425.What should organizations do to reduce the risk of password compromise?

A) Use single-factor authentication

B) Require complex passwords and change them regularly

C) Disable password protection

D) Ignore password policies

426.What is an example of a common check in a security policy for endpoints?

A) User satisfaction surveys

B) Operating system version

C) Network speed

D) Server load

427.What do MDM tools provide to ensure mobile device security?

A) Inconsistent policies

B) Manual updates

C) Full visibility and consistent security

D) Reduced security measures

428.What does the text recommend for maintaining security on mobile devices?

A) Disable updates

B) Use outdated software

C) Utilize MDM tools

D) Ignore security policies

429.What should be done when an endpoint is lost or stolen?

A) Increase internet speed

B) Manually update the device

C) Remotely wipe data or lock the device

D) Disable the device permanently

430.What does full lifecycle asset management include?

A) Only onboarding of assets

B) Only retirement of assets

C) The entire lifecycle of assets from onboarding to retirement

D) Only depreciation of assets

Answers

1. **B) Managed hosting and IaaS**

Explanation:

Managed hosting and IaaS are examples of cloud computing services, as they provide infrastructure resources over the internet rather than hosting them locally.

2. **D) Session hijacking**

Explanation:

While session hijacking is a serious threat, it is typically considered a web-based threat rather than an on-premises threat.

3. **C) Employees**

Explanation:

According to the text, employees are highlighted as the number-one asset for any company. They are indispensable for innovation, product development, and sales.

4. **B) Session hijacking**

Explanation:

Session hijacking involves intercepting traffic between a user and a web resource, allowing attackers to steal session identifiers or manipulate sessions to gain unauthorized access.

5. **B) Stealing sensitive user data**

Explanation:

Phishing attacks aim to deceive users into providing sensitive information such as passwords or credit card numbers.

6. **C) SQL injection**

Explanation:

SQL injection is a common attack technique used to exploit vulnerabilities in web applications by injecting malicious SQL code into input fields.

7. **B) Spyware**

Explanation:

Spyware is a type of malware designed to hide itself and other malicious software on a system, often intercepting and changing operating system processes to avoid detection.

8. **C) To encrypt and obscure the malware code**

Explanation:

Crypters are used to encrypt malware to avoid detection by antivirus software.

9. **C) DoS attack**

Explanation:

A DoS (Denial of Service) attack involves overwhelming a network, server, or system with a flood of traffic or requests, causing it to become slow, unresponsive, or completely unavailable to legitimate users. The goal is to disrupt normal operations, preventing authorized users from accessing the services or resources they need. This type of attack targets the availability aspect of a system's security.

10. A) It requires human interaction to start the infection

Explanation:

Viruses often require user action, such as opening a file, to start the infection process.

11. D) They have unlimited budgets and resources

Explanation:

Nation-state actors typically have significant resources and funding for carrying out sophisticated cyber-attacks.

12. C) Disabling and denying service to legitimate users

Explanation:

The main goal of a DoS attack is to make a service unavailable to its legitimate users.

13. C) XSS attack

Explanation:

Cross-site scripting (XSS) involves injecting malicious scripts into web pages viewed by other users.

14. A) Cross-site scripting

Explanation:

Cross-site scripting is a category, not a specific type. DOM-based, Reflected, and Stored XSS are specific types of XSS attacks.

15. B) NIST Cybersecurity Framework

Explanation:

NIST Cybersecurity Framework is used to collect industry standards for best practices to manage cybersecurity risks. The National Institute of Standards and Technology (NIST) is a part of the U.S. Department of Commerce and a well-known organization.

16. D) To redirect traffic to the attacker's device

Explanation:

ARP spoofing is a technique used in man-in-the-middle attacks to redirect network traffic through the attacker's device, allowing them to intercept and manipulate communications.

17. A) DNS spoofing

Explanation:

DNS spoofing involves corrupting the DNS resolver cache to redirect users to malicious websites controlled by attackers, often used in phishing or malware distribution campaigns.

18. D) By converting HTTPS URLs to HTTP links

Explanation:

In this attack, the attacker intercepts the initial HTTPS request from the client and establishes a connection with the server using HTTPS. However, the attacker then manipulates the traffic to convert HTTPS links to HTTP links before forwarding them to the server. This allows the attacker to intercept and view the unencrypted HTTP traffic while the client and server believe they are communicating securely over HTTPS.

19. C) To install malware on the victim's system

Explanation:

Droppers are a type of malware component designed to install other malicious software on a victim's system, often by delivering payloads or executing commands from remote servers.

20. C) Remote access Trojan (RAT)

Explanation:

Remote access Trojans (RATs) are a type of malware used by attackers to gain unauthorized access to systems, allowing them to control infected devices remotely.

21. C) A DoS attack targets a single host, while a DDoS attack targets multiple hosts

Explanation:

DDoS attacks involve flooding a network or system with requests to disrupt legitimate users' access, often using multiple compromised devices or botnets to generate excessive traffic.

22. C) DoS attack

Explanation:

When an attacker floods a network with ICMP (Internet Control Message Protocol) requests, it's typically referred to as a Denial of Service (DoS) attack. ICMP flood attacks overwhelm the target network with a high volume of ICMP echo request packets, consuming its resources and making it unavailable to legitimate users.

23. B) To verify data integrity
Explanation:

Hashing is primarily used to generate a fixed-size hash value from input data, which is then compared to verify the integrity of the data.

24. B) verify /md5
Explanation:

The 'verify' command with the '/md5' option is used on Cisco devices to generate a hash for verification purposes.

25. C) To convert plaintext to cipher text
Explanation:

Encryption is the process of converting readable data (plaintext) into an unintelligible form (cipher text) to ensure confidentiality.

26. C) One public key and one private key
Explanation:

Asymmetric encryption uses a pair of keys: a public key for encryption and a corresponding private key for decryption.

27. C) To manage digital certificates and keys
Explanation:

Public Key Infrastructure (PKI) is used for managing digital certificates, including their issuance, distribution, and revocation.

28. A) TLS/SSL
Explanation:

TLS/SSL (Transport Layer Security/Secure Sockets Layer) is commonly used for HTTPS to encrypt web communication.

29. C) To establish VPN connections over NAT devices
Explanation:

NAT-T (Network Address Translation Traversal) is used to establish VPN connections over NAT devices by encapsulating ESP packets inside UDP.

30. C) To establish secure connections between devices
Explanation:

Pre-shared keys are used in VPN configurations to establish secure connections between devices by authenticating them during the IKE phase.

31. C) By using digital certificates issued by a Certificate Authority
Explanation:

Certificate-based encryption relies on digital certificates issued by a trusted Certificate Authority for authentication and encryption purposes.

32. C) Site-to-site VPN
Explanation:

A site-to-site VPN securely connects two remote LAN (Local Area Network) sites over the internet, allowing users in one location to access resources in the other location securely. This type of VPN is commonly used to connect branch offices to a central headquarters or to connect geographically dispersed data centers.

33. C) Remote access VPN
Explanation:

A remote access VPN securely connects individual users to a remote LAN, allowing them access to resources and services.

34. C) It enables direct communication between spokes without passing traffic through the hub
Explanation:

DMVPN (Dynamic Multipoint Virtual Private Network) is a VPN technology that allows direct communication between spokes (remote sites) without having to route traffic through a central hub. This feature enhances scalability and efficiency by enabling spoke-to-spoke communication while still maintaining security through encryption and authentication.

35. D) IKEv2
Explanation:

FlexVPN primarily uses IKEv2 (Internet Key Exchange version 2) for configuring various IPsec VPN types.

36. B) Cisco Secure Endpoint (SEP)
Explanation:

Cisco Secure Endpoint provides advanced endpoint protection across various control points, enhancing security.

37. A) To gather and analyze threat information
Explanation:

The main purpose of Security Intelligence (SI) is to collect, analyze, and provide actionable threat information to organizations.

38. B) Cisco Talos Security Intelligence
Explanation:

The Cisco Talos, Security Intelligence team, collects and shares security intelligence across Cisco products and services.

39. C) By collecting, authoring, and sharing security intelligence
Explanation:

Cisco Talos contributes to enhancing security posture by collecting, authoring, and sharing security intelligence to protect against threats.

40. B) Cisco Web Security Appliance (WSA)
Explanation:

Cisco Web Security Appliance analyzes emails for spam, phishing, and malware threats.

41. A) DMVPN
Explanation:

DMVPN enables direct communication between spokes without passing traffic through the hub, making it suitable for hub-and-spoke networks.

42. C) Remote access VPN
Explanation:

Remote access VPN typically involves a web browser portal or a software client for users to connect to a remote LAN.

43. B) They require less configuration and management overhead
Explanation:

sVTI-based VPNs require less configuration and management overhead compared to cryptomap-based VPNs.

44. A) To shape traffic
Explanation:

The policy-map command in configuring an sVTI-based IPsec tunnel is used to shape traffic, controlling its flow and characteristics.

45. B) BeyondCorp
Explanation:

BeyondCorp is a security model created by Google that resembles the zero-trust concept. This model shifts the access control to the users and individual devices from the firewalls and other security devices.

46. A) NetFlow v9

Explanation:

IPFIX (IP Flow Information Export) was created on the basis of NetFlow v9. It is a network flow standard led by the IETF (Internet Engineering Task Force).

47. B) Threat

Explanation: The term threat refers to the potential danger to a resource or asset which can be mitigated by taking preventive measures.

48. C) Vulnerability

Explanation:

Vulnerability refers to the weakness in any system's code, design, or implementation that can be used to gain access to that system.

49. B) Keep cloud-based systems updated with the latest security patches

Explanation:

The primary objective of cloud patch management is to ensure that cloud-based systems are regularly updated with the latest security patches to protect against vulnerabilities and security threats.

50. D) Community Cloud

Explanation:

In a Community Cloud model, infrastructure is shared among multiple organizations with common concerns, such as regulatory compliance or security requirements.

51. **B) Software as a Service**
Explanation:

SaaS refers to Software as a Service, where software applications are hosted by a third-party provider and made available to customers over the internet.

52. **A) Cloud provider**
Explanation:

In a Platform as a Service (PaaS) model, the cloud provider is responsible for managing the underlying infrastructure and application platform, including application patching.

53. **B) NIST SP 800-145**
Explanation:

NIST Special Publication 800-145 defines cloud computing and its essential characteristics according to the National Institute of Standards and Technology (NIST).

54. **A) Cloud access security broker**
Explanation:

Cisco Cloudlock is a cloud access security broker, providing visibility, compliance, and threat protection for cloud applications.

55. **B) On-demand access to cloud-hosted physical and virtual servers, storage, and networking**
Explanation:

Infrastructure as a Service (IaaS) provides customers on-demand access to virtualized resources, including servers, storage, and networking, hosted in the cloud.

56. C) A combination of public cloud and private on-premises resources

Explanation:

A hybrid cloud environment involves the combination of public cloud resources with private on-premises infrastructure, allowing data and applications to be shared between them.

57. A) SaaS

Explanation:

In Software as a Service (SaaS), the cloud provider manages the entire infrastructure and application, with the customer only responsible for the data entered into the system.

58. C) Ease of scaling out

Explanation:

One major benefit of public cloud distributed storage is the ease of scaling out, allowing organizations to dynamically increase storage capacity as needed without significant upfront investment or infrastructure management.

59. B) Private Cloud

Explanation:

Private cloud offers enhanced control, security, and customization options, making it ideal for deploying critical applications and functions where data privacy, compliance, and security are paramount concerns. Cisco often recommends private cloud solutions for organizations seeking to deploy critical workloads in a secure and controlled environment.

60. C) IaaS

Explanation:

In Infrastructure as a Service (IaaS), the cloud provider is responsible for managing the underlying infrastructure, including hardware, virtualization, and operating system maintenance, while customers are responsible for managing applications, data, and middleware.

61. C) 72%
Explanation:

The text states that 72% of IT organizations use a hybrid cloud model.

62. B) It provides a standardized framework for defining cloud computing
Explanation:

NIST 800-145 offers a clear and standardized definition of cloud computing, which helps in understanding and implementing cloud services consistently.

63. C) Development, security, and operations
Explanation:

DevSecOps incorporates security practices into the continuous integration and continuous deployment (CI/CD) pipeline, ensuring security is considered at every stage of development and operations.

64. B) Security of a single customer's infrastructure
Explanation:

Private cloud security is focused on protecting the infrastructure and data of a single organization, ensuring its privacy and security.

65. C) Security and compliance monitoring
Explanation:

Cloud logging is essential for monitoring security events and ensuring compliance with regulations by keeping detailed records of activities.

66. C) Cisco Secure Workload
Explanation:

Cisco Secure Workload assists with managing and applying security patches to cloud workloads.

67. B) Infrastructure shared among multiple organizations with similar goals
Explanation:

A community cloud is used by several organizations that have common goals and requirements, sharing the same infrastructure.

68. A) A server or host with an IP address
Explanation:

In Cisco Secure Workload, a workload typically refers to any entity with an IP address, such as a server or a host, that needs to be monitored and secured.

69. B) On-demand software application access
Explanation:

SaaS provides users with on-demand access to software applications over the Internet, without needing to manage the underlying infrastructure.

70. A) Platform as a Service
Explanation:

PaaS provides a platform allowing customers to develop, run, and manage applications without dealing with the infrastructure.

71. C) IaaS

Explanation:

IaaS gives customers the most control over the infrastructure, including the operating systems, storage, and deployed applications.

72. B) Automated deployment and management of containers
Explanation:

Container orchestration automates the deployment, scaling, and management of containerized applications, improving efficiency and reliability.

73. B) Encrypting them at rest
Explanation:

Encrypting secrets in the CI/CD pipeline ensures they are secure and not accessible to unauthorized users, maintaining the integrity and confidentiality of sensitive information.

74. A) Faster application development
Explanation:

IaaS provides the necessary infrastructure quickly, enabling faster development and deployment of applications without the need for physical hardware.

75. C) Assessing the overall security posture of cloud infrastructure
Explanation:

Cloud security assessments evaluate the security measures in place, identifying vulnerabilities and ensuring that the infrastructure is protected against threats.

76. B) Applications developed to run in cloud environments
Explanation:

Cloud-native applications are specifically designed to take full advantage of cloud computing environments, ensuring scalability, flexibility, and resilience.

77. B) Private Cloud
Explanation:

A private cloud can be scaled according to the needs of the single organization it serves, offering flexibility while maintaining security and control.

78. B) Cloud service models and deployment strategies
Explanation:

NIST SP 500-322 provides detailed guidelines on cloud service models (SaaS, PaaS, IaaS) and deployment strategies (public, private, hybrid, and community clouds).

79. C) IaaS
Explanation:

IaaS offers the customer control over the operating systems, applications, and data, providing the flexibility to manage and configure their infrastructure.

80. C) To secure cloud environments
Explanation:

A CASB like Cisco Cloudlock is used to monitor and secure cloud environments, ensuring compliance and protecting against data breaches and other security threats.

81. B) Private Cloud
Explanation:

Private cloud environments provide dedicated infrastructure and resources for a single organization, offering greater control, security, and customization compared to public cloud deployments. This level of control and security is often essential for critical applications where data privacy, compliance, and performance are top priorities.

82. B) Difficulty in managing security and monitoring solutions
Explanation:

A major challenge of hybrid cloud environments is the difficulty in managing security and monitoring solutions across multiple platforms and ensuring consistent security policies.

83. B) On-demand access to applications without managing the underlying infrastructure
Explanation:

The main benefit of using SaaS (Software as a Service) for organizations is that it provides on-demand access to applications without the need to manage the underlying hardware or software infrastructure.

84. B) PaaS
Explanation:

Platform as a Service (PaaS) is suitable for organizations that want to develop and run applications without the complexity of managing underlying hardware, software, and infrastructure.

85. A) By creating firewalls at the workload level
Explanation:

Cisco Secure Workload helps in application security by creating firewalls at the workload level, providing micro-segmentation, and protecting against threats within cloud environments.

86. A) Software Development Life Cycle
Explanation:

SDLC stands for Software Development Life Cycle, which encompasses the phases of software development from planning and design to deployment and maintenance, emphasizing secure coding practices.

87. B) Using a single solution to track and patch across environments
Explanation:

Cisco recommends using a single solution to track and patch across environments to ensure consistent and efficient patch management in hybrid cloud environments.

88. B) They enhance the visibility of the security posture
Explanation:

A major benefit of cloud security assessments is that they enhance the visibility of the security posture, helping organizations identify vulnerabilities and ensure compliance with security standards.

89. A) Automated data backups
Explanation:

Cisco Secure Workload offers automated data backups as a feature for disaster recovery, ensuring data is regularly backed up and can be restored in case of data loss or breaches.

90. C) XSS

Explanation:

XSS (Cross Site Scripting) is a vulnerability that is present at the client-side (UI) of the application. There are three types of XSS.

- Reflected XSS
- Stored XSS
- DOM-based XSS

91. B) CVE

Explanation:

CVE (Common Vulnerability and Exposure) is a public glossary of vulnerabilities. A CVE ID is assigned to each disclosed vulnerability to identify it.

92. D) Threat intelligence

Explanation:

Threat intelligence refers to the knowledge of an existing or emerging threat to any system, network, or asset by analyzing the collected data to understand the attacker's next steps, behavior, and targets.

93. C) Exploit

Explanation:

The term Exploit refers to the tool, process, or technique to take advantage of a vulnerability in any system. Exploits of the known vulnerabilities can be easily found on the Internet.

94. B) An incident

Explanation:

The term incident refers to any adverse event that can discontinue a business's services or threaten it in any way. It can also be a data breach.

95. B) 802.1x)

Explanation:

802.1x is not used in an IoT network or environment as a communication protocol.

96. A) PaaS

Explanation:

PaaS, Platform as a Service, is a complete development and deployment cloud-based environment. It has resources that allow you to build from simple cloud-based apps to complex and sophisticated enterprise-level apps.

97. Answer: B (Integrity)

Explanation:

Integrity is the original form of any data or configuration. If it is changed or modified, integrity will be lost.

98. C) Availability

Explanation:

Denial-of-service attack impacts any service's availability by slowing it down. It often attacks the server to impact the availability of the service or website.

99. B) White hat

Explanation:

White hat hacker is a type of hacker who works for good causes. Black hat hacker works for the bad causes. Gray hat hacker lies between these two types.

100. D) Ret2Libc

Explanation:

Ransomware is malicious software that restricts access to the system until the ransom is paid to the attacker. Ret2Libc (Ret-to-Libc) is an attack that is usually started with a buffer overflow.

101. C) Chain of custody

Explanation:

Chain of custody refers to the way of documentation and preservation of the evidence from the time of cyber-forensics investigation to the time of presenting it to the court. It ensures the integrity of the evidence and records all of the user activity done against the evidence.

102. C) Because attackers exploit human trust weaknesses
Explanation:

Attackers often target endpoint devices and people due to the ease of exploiting human trust and behavioral weaknesses.

103. C) By stopping known malware and monitoring activity
Explanation:

Cisco Secure Endpoint protects endpoints by blocking known malware and continuously monitoring for suspicious activities.

104. C) Northbound API
Explanation:

The northbound API in SDN allows the controller to communicate with higher-level applications and management systems, exchanging actionable data.

105. C) To facilitate management solutions for automation
Explanation:

Northbound APIs enable the integration of SDN controllers with management and orchestration systems for automation purposes.

106. A) SDN uses a centralized controller for network management
Explanation:

SDN centralizes network management through a controller, unlike traditional networking, which relies on distributed control elements.

107. B) To communicate between controllers and switches
Explanation:

Southbound APIs in SDN facilitate communication between the SDN controller and network devices like switches and routers.

108. D) By pushing intent-based configurations to devices
Explanation:

Cisco DNA Center (DNAC) automates network provisioning by pushing intent-based configurations to network devices.

109. B) Open Platform, API Bound calls
Explanation:

The top level of DNAC's architecture includes open platform and API-bound calls, enabling integrations and extensibility.

110. D) It detects anomalies and alerts administrators
Explanation:

Machine learning in DNAC's assurance feature helps detect network anomalies and provides alerts to administrators for timely intervention.

111. C) It provides a dynamic typing system
Explanation:

Python's dynamic typing and extensive support for libraries make it a powerful language for network automation tasks.

112. C) To interact with external APIs
Explanation:

The requests library in Python is used to make HTTP requests to interact with external APIs.

113. D) By embedding API calls within the script
Explanation:

Python scripts can interact with Cisco Firepower appliances by using API calls to configure and manage the devices.

114. D) Credential theft
Explanation:

Hardcoded credentials in scripts can be easily extracted, leading to credential theft and unauthorized access.

115. B) shlex
Explanation:

The shlex module can be used to sanitize and safely handle user input in Python scripts.

116. B) To define how the SDN controller interacts with the application plane
Explanation:

The eastbound API defines interactions between the SDN controller and application plane for integrating various services and applications.

117. A) By providing SSH protocol implementation
Explanation:

Netmiko uses the SSH protocol to allow Python scripts to communicate with and configure network devices.

118. C) Netmiko
Explanation:

Netmiko is a library built on top of Paramiko to provide easier SSH access for network automation tasks.

119. C) To facilitate interaction with external APIs
Explanation:

The Open Platform, API Bound calls in DNAC enable the integration and interaction with external APIs for enhanced functionality.

120. B) By detecting and alerting on anomalies
Explanation:

DNAC uses its assurance capabilities to detect network anomalies and alert administrators, aiding in troubleshooting.

121. C) argparse
Explanation:

The argparse module is widely used for parsing command-line arguments in Python scripts.

122. C) Community cloud

Explanation:

A community cloud is a type of cloud deployment model whose cloud environment is shared among different organizations. It is very cost-effective, flexible, and scalable. It offers high availability and reliability.

123. C) By stopping known malware and monitoring activity
Explanation:

Cisco Secure Endpoint protects against threats by detecting and blocking known malware and continuously monitoring system activities to identify suspicious behavior.

124. A) Reflected DDoS

Explanation:

In a Reflected DDoS attack, an attacker sends a request (packet) to a source (a random node in the network), and then that source replies with a response packet to the actual victim of the attacker. In this way, the victim gets down and unavailable.

125. A) OWASP

Explanation:

OWASP is a non-profit organization that leads various promotions of cyber security for various organizations. It defines the top 10 vulnerabilities for mobile and web applications that have evolved over the years according to the latest technologies and their security flaws.

126. D) Symmetric

Explanation:

Symmetric cipher uses the same key for encryption and decryption. The private or secret key is used to convert plaintext into a secret code and vice versa.

127. **B) AnyConnect**

Explanation:

You can use the AnyConnect AMP Enabler add-on to help distribute the AMP connector to clients who use AnyConnect for remote access VPN, secure network access, and posture assessments with Cisco's Identity Services Engine and other purposes.

128. B) To integrate with external systems

Explanation:

The eastbound API in network integration is designed to facilitate interaction and integration with external systems and services.

129. B) By providing SSH protocol implementation

Explanation:

Netmiko is a Python library that simplifies SSH management of network devices, allowing scripts to automate device configuration and management over SSH.

130. B) Stream cipher

Explanation:

Stream cipher uses one bit of the key stream at a time to encrypt the plaintext data. It can be asynchronous or synchronous. It is also used in SSL/TLS cipher suite for data-in-transit encryption.

131. A) RSA

Explanation:

RSA (Rivest-Shamir-Adleman) is not a symmetric encryption algorithm. It is a suit of cryptographic algorithms that are used for certain security purposes. It is an asymmetric algorithm. It uses a public key for encryption and a private key for decryption.

132. D) Diffie-Hellman

Explanation:

Diffie-Hellman uses a method of negotiation and establishment of a shared secret keying material (keys) between two devices over an untrusted network. It helps to securely exchange the cryptographic keys over the public network or channel.

133. C) By monitoring and managing cloud application security and compliance

Explanation:

A Cloud Access Security Broker (CASB) like Cisco Cloudlock is designed to enhance the security of cloud applications. It does this by monitoring and managing the security and compliance of cloud applications, ensuring that

data is protected, threats are identified and mitigated, and compliance with regulatory requirements is maintained. This helps organizations securely use cloud services while protecting sensitive data and maintaining control over cloud-based assets.

134. A) Mike's public key

Explanation:

John will use Mike's public key to encrypt the email. If the email is encrypted using Mike's public key, it will be decrypted using Mike's private key and vice versa. The asymmetric key algorithm works on a pair of public and private keys. One key is used for encryption, and the other is for decryption.

135. B) Certificate Authority (CA)

Explanation:

Certificate Authority (CA) is responsible for creating and issuing digital certificates for websites and other entities. It is a trusted organization. A certificate is a small file with data that an entity can verify its authenticity.

136. D) X.500

Explanation:

X.500 is a series of standards focused on the directories' services and organization. It was developed by the Telecommunication Standardization Sector of the International Telecommunication Union.

137. C) requests

Explanation:

The requests library is widely used in Python for making HTTP requests to interact with web APIs.

138. B) FQDN and C) Public key

Explanation:

FQDN (Fully Qualified Domain Name) is needed to configure the SSL certificate, which is present in the digital certificates. The public key of the owner is also present in a digital certificate.

139. C) PKCS #12

Explanation:

PKCS #12 is a format used to store the private and public keys using a password-based key (symmetric) to unlock the data whenever you want to access or use the keys.

140. B) To provide SSH protocol implementation

Explanation:

Netmiko's primary function is to provide an easy-to-use interface for managing network devices over SSH.

141. B) By detecting and alerting on anomalies

Explanation:

DNAC uses machine learning to detect anomalies in network behavior and generate alerts to ensure network reliability and security.

142. A) VXLAN

Explanation:

VXLAN is the most common encapsulation protocol that uses tunneling to provide connectivity in a data center and stretch L2 (layer 2) connections over an underlying L3 (layer 3) network. It creates an overlay network that sits over the physical network. VXLAN encapsulates the MAC address in UDP.

143.C) ast

Explanation:

The ast module in Python processes abstract syntax trees and can be used to analyze and sanitize user inputs.

144. **B) VXLAN Network Identifier (VNID)**

Explanation:

VXLAN Network Identifier (VNID) is a tag that represents a logical segment. Its header includes a 24-bit field, allowing to create more VXLANs than VLANs.

145. **D) East-West traffic**

Explanation:

East-West traffic refers to the network traffic between the containers, servers, and so on. It is basically the traffic from server to server. The name East-West came from the network topologies in which traffic is shown horizontally.

146. **C) Messages in the range of 200**

Explanation:

Messages in the range of 200 occur when an HTTP transaction is successful, i.e., The HTTP 200 OK status comes in an HTTP response after a successful HTTP request.

147. **D) SOAP**

Explanation:

SOAP (Simple Object Access Protocol) is a type of API that exclusively uses XML format to provide messaging services. Microsoft developed it.

148. **C) ast**

Explanation:

The ast (Abstract Syntax Trees) module in Python is used to process and analyze Python code, helping to sanitize and ensure the security of user inputs by parsing and interpreting Python code safely.

149. C) Swagger

Explanation:

Swagger is a modern framework of API documentation. It is a suit of API developer tools. OpenAPI Specification is based upon the Swagger.

150. D) All of the above

Explanation:

RESTCONF supports the following standardized requests;

- PATCH
- PUT
- GET

151. A) XML

Explanation:

NETCONF messages are encoded in an XML structure defined by the NETCONF standard. XML is an easy, useful, and secure format for encoding data.

152. A) IPFIX

Explanation:

IPFIX (IP Flow Information Export) is an extension of NetFlow that provides the ability to collect detailed traffic information in one cache and security information in separate caches, enhancing traffic and security analysis.

153. C) FirePOWER

Explanation:

Cisco's FirePOWER technology provides next-generation security products that offer comprehensive protection across the attack continuum, including advanced threat detection and mitigation.

154. A) Analyze network traffic for signatures matching known cyberattacks
Explanation:

Intrusion Detection Systems (IDSs) are primarily used to analyze network traffic and detect suspicious activities by matching traffic patterns to known attack signatures.

155. A) Cisco ASA 5500-X Series
Explanation:

The Cisco ASA 5500-X Series devices are equipped with both Intrusion Prevention System (IPS) and firewall capabilities, providing robust security features for network protection.

156. A) Transparent mode
Explanation:

In transparent mode, Cisco ASA firewalls do not require IP addresses for their inside and outside interfaces, other than for management purposes, making them effectively invisible to network traffic.

157. A) To act as standalone virtual firewalls with independent configurations
Explanation:

Security contexts in Cisco ASA firewalls allow the creation of multiple virtual firewalls within a single physical firewall, each with its own independent configurations and policies.

158. C) They do not require IP addresses other than for management
Explanation:

Transparent firewalls on Cisco ASA devices operate without requiring IP addresses for the interfaces they protect, except for the management interface.

159. D) Flexible NetFlow
Explanation:

Flexible NetFlow provides more detailed analysis and greater information than Traditional NetFlow by incorporating deep packet inspection (DPI) capabilities.

160. C) It provides user-configurable settings.
Explanation:

Flexible NetFlow is an advanced version of Traditional NetFlow, offering more flexibility and customization options for network traffic analysis. One of its key advantages over Traditional NetFlow is the ability to configure and customize flow records according to specific network monitoring requirements. With Flexible NetFlow, users can define their own flow record formats, including which fields to include and how they are processed, allowing for more detailed and tailored traffic analysis. This flexibility makes Flexible NetFlow a powerful tool for network administrators and analysts to gain insights into network traffic behavior.

161. B) SCTP

Explanation:

SCTP (Stream Control Transmission Protocol) provides a packet transport service designed to support several features beyond TCP or UDP capabilities for IPFIX.

162. **B)** ELK and Graylog

Explanation:

ELK (Elasticsearch, Logstash, Kibana) and Graylog are open-source tools commonly used for analyzing NetFlow data.

163. A) To export flow information to multiple collectors

Explanation:

NetFlow templates define how flow records are formatted and exported, allowing flow information to be sent to multiple collectors.

164. **A) NetFlow v5**

Explanation:

NetFlow v9 is template-based, allowing for flexible and extensible flow data export.

165.**C) At least five minutes**

Explanation:

It is recommended to capture NetFlow v9 packets for at least five minutes to ensure sufficient data collection for analysis.

166. D) To serve as an open standard for flow export

Explanation:

IPFIX (IP Flow Information Export) is an open standard designed to export flow information.

167. B) IPFIX

Explanation:

IPFIX is sometimes referred to as "NetFlow v10," as it is an extension and evolution of NetFlow.

168. C) It provides detailed analysis using deep packet inspection

Explanation:

Flexible NetFlow allows for detailed traffic analysis using deep packet inspection and supports various flow types.

169. B) ip flow-export destination

Explanation:

The command ip flow-export destination is used to configure the destination for exporting NetFlow data on Cisco IOS devices.

170. B) They provide more detailed traffic analysis

Explanation:

Immediate and permanent flows in Flexible NetFlow provide more detailed traffic analysis by capturing specific information as needed.

171. C) show ip flow cache

Explanation:

The command 'show ip flow cache' is used to verify NetFlow operations and statistics on Cisco IOS devices.

172. **C) Cisco ISR routers**

Explanation:

Cisco ISR (Integrated Services Routers) routers support Traditional NetFlow (TNF).

173. C) Cisco ISR routers

Explanation:

Cisco ISR routers also support Flexible NetFlow (FNF).

174. **A) IPFIX is an open standard, while NetFlow v9 is Cisco proprietary**

Explanation:

The primary difference is that IPFIX is an open standard, whereas NetFlow v9 is proprietary to Cisco.

175. B) To provide a description of fields present in future data FlowSets

Explanation:

In NetFlow v9, FlowSets provide a description of the fields present in future data FlowSets.

176. C) Deep packet inspection

Explanation:

Flexible NetFlow uses deep packet inspection to monitor specific information in packets and allow for different flow types.

177. D) To provide a packet transport service with additional features

Explanation:

SCTP in IPFIX provides a packet transport service with features beyond those offered by TCP or UDP.

178. B) ip flow-export destination

Explanation:

The command ip flow-export destination is used to configure the export of NetFlow data on Cisco IOS devices.

179. **D) IPv6 flow** information

Explanation:

NetFlow v9 captures IPv6 flow information, which Traditional NetFlow does not support.

180. **B) They allow for future enhancements without fundamental changes**

Explanation:

NetFlow templates allow for future enhancements in flow data export without requiring fundamental changes to the protocol.

181. **C) It is an open standard supported by many networking vendors**

Explanation:

The primary advantage of IPFIX over NetFlow v9 is that it is an open standard supported by many networking vendors.

182. **D) To serve as an open standard for flow export**

Explanation:

NetFlow templates are primarily used to define the format for exporting flow data, allowing for a standardized representation of network traffic information across different NetFlow-enabled devices and applications.

183. **C) At least five minutes**

Explanation:

It is recommended to capture NetFlow v9 packets for at least five minutes to ensure that an adequate number of flow records and template packets are captured, facilitating proper decoding and analysis.

184. B) ip flow-export destination
Explanation:

The ip flow-export destination command is used to configure the destination where NetFlow data is exported on Cisco IOS devices.

185. C) They provide more detailed traffic analysis
Explanation:

The key advantage of using Flexible NetFlow's immediate and permanent flows is that they provide more detailed traffic analysis compared to traditional methods.

186. B) DEVNET

Explanation: DEVNET is a Cisco developers program that helps IT professionals write applications and integrate with Cisco products, APIs, and platforms. This certification validates the skills of DevOps Engineers, software developers, and automation specialists.

187. C) YANG model

Explanation: The YANG data model consists of modules and sub-modules that define state data and configuration, RPCs, and notifications for NETCONF-based operations.

188. C) To provide a packet transport service with additional features
Explanation:

The main purpose of Stream Control Transmission Protocol (SCTP) in IPFIX is to provide a packet transport service with additional features such as reliability, message fragmentation, and multihoming support.

189. A) show ip flow cache
Explanation:

The show ip flow cache command is used to verify NetFlow operations and statistics on Cisco IOS devices, displaying information about the flow cache.

190. D) Authentication by knowledge
Explanation:

Authentication by knowledge is a type of authentication in which you know something such as a secret that no one else can get to know. It can be a password, pin code, or answer to a security question.

191. B) One-time passcode (OTP)
Explanation:

One-time passcode (OTP) is a set of attributes that can be used if you want to prove a subject's identity only once and expires after using it. It is sent to the user's device. If it is captured, no one can use it after your usage.

192. B) Detailed traffic analysis and deep packet inspection
Explanation:

Flexible NetFlow provides capabilities for detailed traffic analysis, including deep packet inspection (DPI) for advanced monitoring and analysis.

193. A) Normal, immediate, and permanent
Explanation:

Flexible NetFlow supports three types of flow monitoring: normal, immediate, and permanent.

194. C) Flow records
Explanation:

Flow records in Flexible NetFlow allow for the definition and customization of the specific information to be captured from IP traffic.

195. C) By configuring flow monitors with ACLs
Explanation:

Flexible NetFlow can be configured to capture specific types of traffic by configuring flow monitors with ACLs (Access Control Lists).

196. A) Partitioning of the firewall into virtual firewalls
Explanation:

Cisco ASA security contexts allow for the partitioning of the firewall into multiple virtual firewalls, each with its own independent configurations and policies.

197. C) Routed and inline mode
Explanation:

Cisco FTD (Firepower Threat Defense) devices support deployment in routed and inline modes, providing flexibility in network deployment scenarios.

198. C) Inline mode
Explanation:

Inline mode of Cisco FTD operates as both a next-generation firewall (NGFW) and next-generation intrusion prevention system (NGIPS).

199. C) To identify trends and anomalies in network behavior
Explanation:

The primary purpose of NetFlow data analysis is to identify trends and anomalies in network behavior, aiding in network troubleshooting, optimization, and security monitoring.

200. A) SiLK, ELK, and Graylog
Explanation:

SiLK, ELK (Elasticsearch, Logstash, Kibana), and Graylog are open-source tools commonly used for analyzing NetFlow data.

201. B) By avoiding the reinvention of products for each new NetFlow feature
Explanation:

NetFlow templates benefit companies developing NetFlow applications by allowing them to avoid reinventing products for each new NetFlow feature, facilitating interoperability and scalability.

202. B) VLANs
Explanation:

VLANs (Virtual Local Area Networks) can spread across multiple switches and treat each VLAN as its own subnet or broadcast domain, enhancing network segmentation and management.

203. C) Reducing broadcast domains
Explanation:

The primary benefit of VLANs is reducing broadcast domains, which helps in improving network performance and management.

204. C) Switch behaving like a hub
Explanation:

A potential consequence of MAC address flooding attacks is that the switch behaves like a hub, broadcasting all received packets to all ports, which can lead to network congestion and security vulnerabilities.

205. C) Port Security
Explanation:

Port Security is used to prevent MAC address attacks by limiting and securing the MAC addresses allowed to access specific switch ports.

206. D) To intercept sensitive data from the network
Explanation:

The purpose of DHCP Rogue Attack is to intercept sensitive data from the network by posing as a rogue DHCP server and distributing unauthorized IP addresses to unsuspecting clients.

207. C) Dynamic ARP Inspection
Explanation:

Dynamic ARP Inspection is a security feature that protects networks against Man-in-the-Middle ARP spoofing attacks by verifying ARP packets before they are forwarded.

208. D) A form of Man-in-the-Middle attack
Explanation:

ARP Spoofing is a form of Man-in-the-Middle attack where an attacker sends fake Address Resolution Protocol (ARP) messages to associate their MAC address with the IP address of another network device, allowing them to intercept and manipulate network traffic.

209. C) Data plane
Explanation:

The data plane of a network device is responsible for forwarding data packets between network interfaces.

210. A) To manage the traffic flow of control plane packets

Explanation:

Control Plane Policing (CoPP) is used to manage the traffic flow of control plane packets to protect the control plane from being overwhelmed by excessive or malicious traffic.

211. D) To increase the security of the network
Explanation:

IP options primarily serve to increase the security of the network by allowing for various options such as timestamping, record routes, etc.

212.B) no ip redirects

Explanation:

This command disables the transmission of ICMP redirects, which are messages used by routers to inform hosts of a better route for a particular destination.

213.B) Unicast RPF

Explanation:

Unicast Reverse Path Forwarding (Unicast RPF) is a feature used to verify the source address of a forwarded packet by checking if the route to the source address is the same as the route used to forward the packet.

214. A) Loose mode

Explanation:

In cases of asymmetric routing, the loose mode of Unicast RPF is preferred as it checks if the source IP address of the packet has a route back to the interface that received the packet.

215.C) Management plane traffic

Explanation:

Management Plane Protection (MPP) restricts access to and from the management plane of a network device to prevent unauthorized access and attacks targeting the management plane.

216. A) By increasing broadcast domains

Explanation:

VLANs reduce security risks by increasing broadcast domains, thus limiting the scope of broadcast storms and reducing the potential impact of broadcast-based attacks.

217.C) MAC Address Flooding Attack

Explanation:

MAC Address Flooding Attack involves flooding a switch with fake MAC addresses to overload the switch's MAC address table, potentially leading to a denial of service or enabling a Man-in-the-Middle attack.

218. C) Port Security

Explanation:

Port Security is a security feature that prevents a network attacker from sending large numbers of Ethernet frames with forged source MAC addresses by limiting the number of MAC addresses allowed on a port.

219. C) SAML

Explanation:

SAML stands for Security Assertion Markup Language, is an open-source project that is used in various single sign-on (SSO) implementations and is

mainly used for exchanging authorization and authentication data between two peers (identity providers).

220. A) ARP Spoofing

Explanation:

Dynamic ARP Inspection (DAI) protects against ARP Spoofing, a type of attack where attackers send falsified ARP messages over a local area network to link their MAC address with the IP address of a legitimate device or gateway.

221.B) To develop, test, and deploy code rapidly and reliably
Explanation:

A CI/CD pipeline is used to automate the integration, testing, and deployment processes in software development, ensuring rapid and reliable delivery of code changes.

222. B) The ability to increase or decrease resources as needed
Explanation:

Scalability in cloud computing refers to the capacity to dynamically adjust resources to meet changing demands.

223. A) The integration of development, security, and operations
Explanation:

DevSecOps integrates security practices into the DevOps process, ensuring that security is a shared responsibility throughout the development lifecycle.

224. B) Offering on-demand access to physical and virtual infrastructure resources
Explanation:

The primary function of Infrastructure as a Service (IaaS) is to provide on-demand access to computing, storage, and networking resources.

225. B) An authorization model

Explanation:

An authorization model defines permissions and access rights to someone. Authorization refers to the specific rights granted to someone to access or use a resource.

226. D) Community Cloud

Explanation:

A community cloud is shared by multiple organizations with similar requirements, allowing them to collaborate on shared infrastructure.

227. C) By offering tools to secure cloud applications and data

Explanation:

A CASB like Cisco Cloudlock provides security tools to protect cloud applications and data from threats and ensure compliance.

228. B) To enhance application security and compliance

Explanation:

Cisco Secure Workload focuses on improving security and compliance for applications in cloud environments.

229. D) Efficient application deployment and scaling

Explanation:

Containers facilitate the efficient deployment and scaling of applications, making it easier to manage and move applications across different environments.

230. C) Hybrid Cloud
Explanation:

A hybrid cloud combines private and public cloud infrastructures, allowing data and applications to be shared between them.

231. C) It delivers virtualized computing resources over the internet
Explanation:

The IaaS model provides virtualized computing resources such as servers, storage, and networking over the internet.

232. C) Cloud security and compliance
Explanation:

Cisco Cloudlock focuses on securing data, applications, and services in the cloud, ensuring compliance with regulatory requirements.

233. D) 802.1X
Explanation:

802.1X is a standard through which a network access device (switch or wireless access point) can enable port-based access control, i.e., it allows traffic to access the port only after authorization and authentication. There are three main roles in an 802.1X enabled network;

- Authentication Server
- Authenticator
- Supplicant

234. B) The ability to automatically increase or decrease IT resources as needed
Explanation:

Elasticity in cloud computing refers to the ability to dynamically provision and deprovision IT resources to meet changing demand.

235. B) Enhancing security for cloud-native applications
Explanation:

Cisco Secure Workload focuses on enhancing security for cloud-native applications by providing visibility and enforcing security policies.

236. C) IaaS
Explanation:

In the IaaS model, the provider manages the underlying infrastructure and virtualization, while the customer manages the operating system, applications, and data.

237. B) They are optimized for cloud environments, allowing for better scalability and performance
Explanation:

Cloud-native applications are designed to leverage cloud computing features, offering better scalability, resilience, and performance.

238. B) A Cloud Access Security Broker that monitors and secures cloud applications
Explanation:

A CASB enhances cloud security by monitoring and securing the use of cloud applications and ensuring compliance with security policies.

239. B) Private Cloud
Explanation:

A private cloud provides the highest level of physical control over infrastructure, as it is dedicated to a single organization.

240. B) Simplified deployment and management of applications
Explanation:

PaaS provides a platform that simplifies the development, deployment, and management of applications without needing to manage the underlying infrastructure.

241. B) Applications specifically designed to take advantage of cloud computing models
Explanation:

Cloud-native applications are designed to exploit the benefits of cloud computing, such as elasticity, scalability, and resilience.

242. B) PaaS
Explanation:

PaaS is ideal for organizations that want to develop, run, and manage applications without handling the underlying hardware and software infrastructure.

243. B) Automated deployment, scaling, and management of containerized applications
Explanation:

Orchestration refers to the automated management of containerized applications, including their deployment, scaling, and operation.

244. C) Monitoring and analyzing security events and compliance
Explanation:

A cloud logging solution primarily focuses on collecting, monitoring, and analyzing log data to ensure security, compliance, and operational insights.

245. A) SaaS
Explanation:

Software as a Service (SaaS) offers the highest level of abstraction, providing fully managed software applications to end-users over the internet.

246. C) Enhancing security and compliance through visibility and segmentation
Explanation:

Cisco Secure Workload enhances security and compliance by providing detailed visibility and segmentation of application workloads in cloud environments.

247. A) Continuous Integration/Continuous Deployment
Explanation:

CI/CD stands for Continuous Integration and Continuous Deployment, which are practices aimed at improving software development and delivery processes through automation.

248. B) Private Cloud
Explanation:

A private cloud involves resources dedicated to a single organization, which can be hosted either on-premises or by a third-party provider.

249. B) It combines the scalability of public cloud with the security of private cloud
Explanation:

A hybrid cloud model offers the flexibility and scalability of public cloud services while maintaining the security and control of a private cloud.

250. B) To evaluate and enhance the security posture of cloud infrastructure
Explanation:

A cloud security assessment aims to identify vulnerabilities and improve the overall security of cloud infrastructure and services.

251. B) Private Cloud
Explanation:

Private Cloud is ideal for organizations with highly sensitive data and stringent security requirements because it offers dedicated infrastructure and greater control over security measures.

252. C) Implementing a Cloud Access Security Broker (CASB)
Explanation:

Cisco recommends implementing a Cloud Access Security Broker (CASB) to ensure secure access to cloud services. CASBs provide visibility, compliance, and data security across multiple cloud services.

253. C) Enhanced scalability and portability of applications
Explanation:

The primary advantage of using containers for application deployment is their enhanced scalability and portability, allowing applications to be easily moved across different environments and scaled as needed.

254. A) Multiple users sharing a single cloud resource
Explanation:

In the context of cloud computing, multi-tenancy refers to multiple users sharing a single cloud resource, such as servers or storage infrastructure.

255. C) To provide cloud security and compliance management

Explanation:

The main function of Cisco Cloudlock in a cloud environment is to provide cloud security and compliance management, including threat protection, data loss prevention, and compliance monitoring.

256. **B) Simplified software deployment and maintenance**

Explanation:

A significant benefit of using a Software as a Service (SaaS) model is simplified software deployment and maintenance, as the service provider handles software updates, patches, and maintenance tasks.

257. **C) Hybrid Cloud**

Explanation:

Hybrid Cloud allows an organization to maintain control over sensitive data while leveraging public cloud resources for scalability, providing a balance between security and flexibility.

258. **C) To provide security and visibility for cloud-native applications**

Explanation:

One of the primary functions of Cisco Secure Workload is to provide security and visibility for cloud-native applications, ensuring that they are protected from threats and compliance risks.

259. **D) Contextual information, including application, user, URL, payload, etc.**

Explanation:

The action taken by ACP rules in Cisco FMC is determined by contextual information, including application, user, URL, payload, etc., not just source or destination IP addresses.

260. A) It uses URL lists for filtering
Explanation:

URL filtering in Firepower Management Center uses URL lists for filtering and categorizing web traffic based on defined policies.

261. D) Malware protection
Explanation:

Malware protection is a feature of the Firepower system that requires additional licensing for protecting against malicious software.

262. D) Intrusion Prevention System (IPS)
Explanation:

Intrusion Prevention System (IPS) provides network visibility throughout the full attack continuum, helping to detect and prevent network-based attacks in real time.

263. C) Three
Explanation:

SNMPv3 provides three security models: SNMPv3 User-based Security Model (USM), SNMPv3 View-based Access Control Model (VACM), and SNMPv3 Message Processing.

264. B) To protect information from unauthorized access
Explanation:

The primary objective of access controls is to protect information from unauthorized access by enforcing policies that govern who can access what resources.

265. A) aaa new-model
Explanation:

The command aaa new-model activates AAA (Authentication, Authorization, and Accounting) features on Cisco devices, enabling centralized control over user access and permissions.

266. B) Discretionary Access Control
Explanation:

DAC stands for Discretionary Access Control in access control mechanisms, which allows users to control access to their own objects and resources based on their discretion

267. C) Three
Explanation:

ISAKMP (Internet Security Association and Key Management Protocol) negotiation consists of three phases: Phase 1 for establishing a secure channel, Phase 2 for setting up IPsec security associations, and Phase 3 for creating a secure connection between peers.

268. C) Both encryption and authentication
Explanation:

IPsec provides both encryption and authentication for the transmission of sensitive information over unprotected networks, ensuring data confidentiality, integrity, and authenticity.

269. A) VPN termination
Explanation:

The primary function of the Cisco AnyConnect client is VPN termination, allowing users to establish secure connections to remote networks over the internet.

270. B) copy tftp flash
Explanation:

The command copy tftp flash is used to upload the AnyConnect image to a router's flash memory from a TFTP server.

271.A) Using the crypto generate rsa command
Explanation:

RSA keys are generated on a Cisco router using the command crypto generate rsa.

272. A) crypto pki trustpoint
Explanation:

The command crypto pki trustpoint is used to create a trustpoint on a Cisco router for managing certificate-based authentication in VPN configurations.

273. C) To establish secure communication
Explanation:

The purpose of a trustpoint in VPN configuration is to establish secure communication by managing certificate-based authentication between VPN peers.

274. B) UDP
Explanation:

NTP (Network Time Protocol) uses UDP (User Datagram Protocol) for time synchronization between devices.

275. C) SNMPv3
Explanation:

SNMPv3 provides secure access to devices by encrypting and authenticating data packets, ensuring confidentiality, integrity, and authenticity of SNMP communications.

276. D) Authentication, encryption, and message integrity
Explanation:

SNMPv3 provides authentication, encryption, and message integrity for securing SNMP communications.

277. A) To control access to network resources
Explanation:

ACLs (Access Control Lists) in VPN configuration are used to control access to network resources by specifying which traffic is permitted or denied through the VPN tunnel.

278. D) To prevent NAT traversal issues
Explanation:

Configuring NAT (Network Address Translation) in VPN tunnels helps prevent NAT traversal issues by ensuring that traffic is properly translated and routed between private and public networks.

279. B) To connect multiple branch offices securely
Explanation:

The primary function of site-to-site IPsec VPN tunnels is to connect multiple branch offices securely over the internet, forming a secure network between geographically dispersed locations.

280. B) Using ISAKMP and ESP
Explanation:

IPsec VPN tunnels are encrypted and authenticated using ISAKMP (Internet Security Association and Key Management Protocol) for negotiation and ESP (Encapsulating Security Payload) for encapsulation and encryption of data.

281. D) To verify the authenticity of NTP servers
Explanation:

The primary purpose of NTP authentication is to verify the authenticity of NTP servers, ensuring that time synchronization is performed with trusted and authenticated sources.

282. B) Protect end users from connecting to malicious websites
Explanation:

The primary function of a web proxy server is to protect end users from connecting to malicious websites by intercepting and filtering web requests before they reach the end user's device.

283. D) RELP
Explanation:

RELP (Reliable Event Logging Protocol) is recommended for real-time visibility into logs because it ensures the reliable delivery of log messages, making it suitable for critical logging applications where message loss is not acceptable.

284. C) Correlating logs from different infrastructures and application sources
Explanation:

The benefit of centralized logging is the ability to correlate logs from different infrastructures and application sources, allowing for comprehensive analysis and identification of security events and anomalies.

285. B) Transporting logs using an API
Explanation:

Log replication involves transporting logs using an API to replicate log data from one location to another, typically from distributed sources to a centralized logging system.

286. A) Log analysis and storage
Explanation:

The core components of any security program related to logs include log analysis and storage, which involve analyzing log data for security events and storing logs securely for compliance and forensic purposes.

287. C) Storage scalability and log retention period
Explanation:

The main consideration when configuring log storage is storage scalability and log retention period, ensuring that the storage solution can accommodate the volume of logs generated and retain them for the required duration.

288. B) By hiding the user's IP address
Explanation:

A web proxy improves user privacy by hiding the user's IP address from the websites they visit, thereby adding a layer of anonymity and protecting their identity online.

289. B) To improve security and privacy
Explanation:

The primary function of a web proxy server is to improve security and privacy. A web proxy server sits between the end user and the Internet, intercepting web requests from the end-user client. It can block access to

websites that are not in compliance with an organization's acceptable use policy (AUP), thereby improving security.

290. C) Blocking access to non-conformant websites
Explanation:

URL filtering in a web proxy involves blocking access to non-conformant websites based on predefined policies, ensuring that users cannot access websites that violate acceptable use policies or pose security risks.

291. B) Allowing access required for the application to function while blocking everything else
Explanation:

Application whitelisting allows access required for the application to function while blocking everything else, ensuring that only trusted applications are allowed to execute on the system, thereby reducing the attack surface.

292. C) Block-list policy
Explanation:

A traditional security policy typically implements a block-list policy, where specific entities, such as IP addresses, domains, or applications, are explicitly blocked, while everything else is allowed by default.

293. B) By monitoring application behavior over time
Explanation:

A baseline of normal activity in an application can be established by monitoring application behavior over time, identifying patterns and anomalies, and defining what constitutes normal behavior for the application.

294. B) Process business logic
Explanation:

The role of the application server in a distributed application is to process business logic, handling user requests, and executing application-specific operations.

295. A) 80 and 443
Explanation:

Ports 80 and 443 are typically associated with the web server in the sample distributed application, where port 80 is used for HTTP traffic and port 443 is used for HTTPS traffic.

296. C) Filtering and extracting useful information
Explanation:

Defining logging levels allows for filtering and extracting useful information from log messages, enabling administrators to focus on relevant events and prioritize actions based on their severity.

297. A) Using documentation and operating system tools like netstat and lsof
Explanation:

Network services dependencies in a large distributed application environment can be identified using documentation and operating system tools like netstat and lsof, which provide information about active network connections and open files.

298. B) Application verbosity and storage requirements
Explanation:

When configuring the storage method for logs, factors such as application verbosity (amount of log data generated) and storage requirements (capacity

and performance) should be considered to ensure efficient and effective log management.

299. C) TCP
Explanation:

TCP (Transmission Control Protocol) is recommended for transmitting logs to ensure reliability, as it provides connection-oriented communication, error detection, and retransmission of lost packets, ensuring that log messages are delivered reliably.

300. B) To correlate logs from various sources for a holistic view
Explanation:

It's important to have a centralized logging system to correlate logs from various sources for a holistic view of security events and network activity, enabling efficient analysis, detection, and response to security incidents.

301. B) By using vulnerability analysis comparing files against known vulnerabilities
Explanation:

Vulnerabilities in installed software can be detected by performing vulnerability analysis, which involves comparing files against a known set of vulnerabilities to identify potential security weaknesses.

302. A) Reliable Event Logging Protocol
Explanation:

RELP stands for Reliable Event Logging Protocol, which is used for securely transmitting logs with reliability and data integrity.

303. A) To define baselines and understand patterns and anomalies
Explanation:

The primary goal of log analysis is to define baselines, understand regular patterns, and identify anomalies in log data to detect security incidents or troubleshoot issues effectively.

304. B) They should not depend on the application hosting infrastructure
Explanation:

An important aspect of application security solutions is that they should not depend on the application hosting infrastructure, ensuring consistent security controls regardless of where the applications are hosted.

305. B) Categorizing attributes to determine website risk
Explanation:

The primary function of Cisco Secure Web Appliance's web reputation engine is to categorize attributes related to web traffic to assess the risk associated with websites and determine whether they should be blocked.

306. B) By ensuring all web activity is logged
Explanation:

Centralized logging helps with compliance requirements by ensuring that all web activity is logged, facilitating auditing, analysis, and meeting regulatory requirements.

307. B) Monitoring network services and identifying dependencies
Explanation:

Netstat and lsof tools are used in application security for monitoring network services and identifying dependencies, helping administrators understand the network traffic and potential security risks.

308. B) Reliability and data integrity

Explanation:

A key benefit of using TCP for log transmission is its reliability and data integrity, ensuring that log data is transmitted securely without loss or corruption.

309. C) They should be written to files
Explanation:

Logs on local disks should be written to files by default to record system events and activities for auditing, troubleshooting, and analysis purposes.

310. A) Web Cache Communication Protocol
Explanation:

WCCP stands for Web Cache Communication Protocol, which is used for communication between web caches (proxy servers) and routers to redirect web traffic.

311. B) UDP
Explanation:

UDP (User Datagram Protocol) is generally less reliable for log transmission compared to TCP, as it does not guarantee delivery or ensure data integrity.

312.A) Improved web performance and reduced outgoing bandwidth
Explanation:

Proxy cache in Cisco Secure Web Appliance improves web performance and reduces outgoing bandwidth by caching content from popular websites, reducing the need to fetch content from the original servers repeatedly.

313. B) To enable real-time visibility and monitoring
Explanation:

It is important to configure applications to write log events directly to a centralized log management system to enable real-time visibility and monitoring of log data, facilitating rapid detection and response to security incidents.

314.B) Allow-list policy
Explanation:

An allow-list policy explicitly allows required access while blocking everything else by default, adhering to the principle of least privilege and enhancing security.

315.B) Caching content from popular websites
Explanation:

A primary function of a web proxy server in terms of performance is caching content from popular websites, which reduces latency and improves response times for subsequent requests.

316. A) By hiding the end user's IP address
Explanation:

The Cisco Secure Web Appliance protects user privacy by hiding the end user's IP address, ensuring anonymity and enhancing privacy while browsing the web.

317.B) Define specific logging levels
Explanation:

To reduce information overload and disk storage consumption in logging, specific logging levels can be defined to filter and extract useful information while avoiding unnecessary log entries.

318. B) Real-time data visualization tools

Explanation:

The centralized logging system should provide real-time data visualization tools for effective log analysis, allowing administrators to identify patterns, anomalies, and security incidents promptly.

319. B) Processing business logic
Explanation:

The primary role of an application server in a distributed application is to process business logic, handling data processing, and executing application-specific functions.

320. B) Behavior monitoring over time
Explanation:

Behavior monitoring over time helps establish a baseline of normal application activity by observing and analyzing how an application behaves under normal conditions, facilitating the detection of abnormal behavior indicative of security threats.

321. B) All logs, including applications, networking devices, workstations, and servers
Explanation:

All types of logs, including those from applications, networking devices, workstations, and servers, should be stored in a centralized repository for comprehensive monitoring, analysis, and compliance purposes.

322. B) Transport Layer Security
Explanation:

TLS stands for Transport Layer Security, which is a cryptographic protocol used to secure communications over a network by providing encryption, data integrity, and authentication.

323. D) UDP
Explanation:

UDP (User Datagram Protocol) is not recommended for log transportation as it does not provide reliability, data integrity, or congestion control, making it less suitable for transmitting critical log data.

324. B) Correlation of logs for a holistic view
Explanation:

The primary advantage of centralized logging is the ability to correlate logs from different sources, providing a holistic view of the environment and facilitating comprehensive analysis and threat detection.

325. B) Web reputation engine
Explanation:

The Cisco Secure Web Appliance's web reputation engine categorizes attributes to determine website risk, assessing the trustworthiness and security of websites to block potentially harmful content.

326. B) Type of applications and their logging verbosity
Explanation:

When defining the log retention period, consideration should be given to the type of applications and their logging verbosity, as more verbose logging may require longer retention periods and vice versa.

327. B) By caching content from popular websites
Explanation:

Proxy servers improve web performance by caching content from popular websites, reducing latency and response times by serving cached content to users instead of fetching it from the original servers.

328. A) To ensure data integrity and reliability
Explanation:

It is important to use a reliable protocol like RELP or TCP for log transmission to ensure data integrity and reliability, ensuring that log data reaches its destination accurately and securely.

329. C) By blocking access to websites not in conformance with the acceptable use policy
Explanation:

A web proxy server controls internet access by blocking access to websites that are not in conformance with the acceptable use policy (AUP), enforcing security policies, and mitigating risks associated with unauthorized web browsing.

330. A) To configure automatic proxy settings for the client
Explanation:

A PAC (Proxy Auto-Configuration) file is used to configure automatic proxy settings for client browsers, directing web traffic through the proxy server based on predefined rules and conditions.

331. C) Cisco Secure Endpoint
Explanation:

AMP for Endpoints has been rebranded to Cisco Secure Endpoint, reflecting its integration into Cisco's broader security portfolio.

332. B) Detecting and investigating suspicious activities on endpoints
Explanation:

EDR solutions focus on detecting and investigating suspicious activities on endpoints to provide advanced threat detection and response capabilities.

333. **D) Data encryption**
Explanation:

While data encryption is important for security, it is not a primary function of an EDR solution, which focuses on threat detection, response, and investigation.

334. **B) Endpoint protection (EPP)**
Explanation:

EPP solutions are designed to protect endpoints against exploits and attacks, providing comprehensive security.

335. **B) In the cloud**
Explanation:

Cisco Secure Endpoint leverages cloud-based processing to provide scalable and efficient threat detection and response.

336. **D) Dynamic file analysis**
Explanation:

Dynamic file analysis in Cisco Secure Endpoint uses cloud intelligence to monitor and analyze files, scripts, and network activities.

337. **B) To monitor and analyze files for changing threat levels**
Explanation:

Retrospective security continuously monitors and analyzes files to detect changes in threat levels, providing ongoing protection.

338. **B) Fuzzy fingerprinting**
Explanation:

Fuzzy fingerprinting helps block malware families that use polymorphism by identifying and matching similar malicious patterns.

339. **A) Endpoint IoCs**
Explanation:

Endpoint Indicators of Compromise (IoCs) use cloud-based pattern recognition to detect and highlight suspicious activities on endpoints.

340. **B) Dynamic file analysis**
Explanation:

Dynamic file analysis correlates samples with a vast database of other samples and artifacts to enhance threat detection accuracy.

341.**A) Creating application allow and block lists**
Explanation:

Custom detections allow administrators to create specific allow and block lists for applications based on organizational policies.

342. **B) Blocked Applications**
Explanation:

The Blocked Applications feature prevents the execution of specific programs without quarantining them, maintaining system integrity.

343. **C) Wildcard exclusion**
Explanation:

Wildcard exclusions allow for the flexible exclusion of files or paths using wildcards, covering a broad range of potential targets.

344. B) Downloading, editing, and re-uploading the file
Explanation:

To edit an uploaded IP list, administrators must download the file, make necessary changes, and then re-upload it.

345. B) Stops the execution of programs on hosts
Explanation:

The Blocked Applications feature halts the execution of programs deemed suspicious or harmful, preventing potential threats.

346. A) Cisco-maintained exclusions
Explanation:

Cisco-maintained exclusions are updated by Cisco and pushed to endpoints to ensure up-to-date threat prevention.

347. D) To prevent all internet traffic
Explanation:

Endpoint security aims to protect devices and data, not to block all internet traffic, which would impede normal operations.

348. B) By creating allow lists
Explanation:

Allow lists in Cisco Secure Endpoint ensure that trusted, custom-built applications are not mistakenly quarantined.

349. C) Signature-based engine
Explanation:

A signature-based engine provides on-disk malware detection by identifying known malware patterns and signatures.

350. C) Scanning post-compromise indicators across multiple endpoints

Explanation:

Endpoint IoCs help in scanning and identifying signs of compromise across multiple endpoints to detect and respond to threats.

351. B) Dynamic file analysis

Explanation:

Dynamic file analysis includes detailed reports and videos of file behavior during detonation to assist in threat analysis.

352. B) Block lists and allow lists

Explanation:

Organizations can supplement Cisco's threat intelligence by creating and managing custom blocks and allow lists for specific needs.

353. C) Rapid updates leveraging cloud resources

Explanation:

Cloud-based malware detection benefits from rapid updates and scalability, leveraging extensive cloud resources for timely threat responses.

354. B) A powerful threat-hunting capability

Explanation:

The Endpoint IoCs feature enhances threat-hunting capabilities by identifying and investigating indicators of compromise across endpoints.

355. A) By using the Threat exclusion set
Explanation:

Organizations can manage the exclusion of specific detections by threat name through the Threat exclusion set, which allows them to specify exclusions based on the names of identified threats, enhancing flexibility in security management.

356. B) Device flow correlation
Explanation:

Device flow correlation blocks malicious IP communications by analyzing and managing network traffic flows.

357. C) By creating an exclusion set
Explanation:

Organizations can create exclusion sets to manage the execution of critical but vulnerable programs, ensuring they are not blocked unnecessarily.

358. C) Exclusion sets
Explanation:

Exclusion sets can be utilized to resolve conflicts with other security products by excluding specific detections or files from being flagged as threats, thus preventing unnecessary conflicts or false positives.

359. C) Both a and b
Explanation:

To create and name a list of allowed or blocked applications in Cisco Secure Endpoint, organizations typically need to upload the application and enter its SHA-256 hash for identification purposes.

360. B) Behavioral indicators

Explanation:

Dynamic file analysis in Cisco Secure Endpoint leverages behavioral indicators to analyze the behavior of files in real-time, allowing the system to identify potentially malicious activities and take appropriate action.

361. **B) Automatically by policy**
Explanation:

Updates to Cisco-maintained exclusions are automatically pushed to endpoints by policy, ensuring that the latest exclusion rules and definitions are consistently applied across the organization's security infrastructure.

362. **A) Application control list**
Explanation:

Cisco Secure Endpoint can create a custom detection list known as the "Application control list" to manage applications by specifying which ones are allowed or blocked based on organizational policies.

363. **C) To protect against threats like malware and ransomware**
Explanation:

Endpoint security is essential for users who access the Internet while offline to protect against threats like malware and ransomware, as they may be more vulnerable to attacks without the protection of network-based security measures.

364. **D) By performing dynamic file analysis**
Explanation:

Large file or database performance issues in Cisco Secure Endpoint can be mitigated by performing dynamic file analysis, which allows the system to analyze files in real-time without compromising performance.

365. B) Cloud-based detection and analysis
Explanation:

Secure Endpoint remains lightweight while performing various functions due to its cloud-based detection and analysis capabilities, which offload processing tasks to remote servers, reducing the burden on endpoint devices.

366. C) Custom detections
Explanation:

Custom detections in Cisco Secure Endpoint help with proactive threat hunting by allowing organizations to create specific detection rules tailored to their unique security requirements, enabling the identification of potential threats before they escalate.

367. C) In an audit log
Explanation:

Changes to IP lists in Cisco Secure Endpoint are typically logged in as an audit log, providing a record of modifications made to the lists for security and compliance purposes.

368. D) To monitor network activity
Explanation:

Custom detections in Secure Endpoint offer the benefit of monitoring network activity by allowing organizations to create specific detection rules tailored to their network environment, enhancing visibility and threat detection capabilities.

369. B) Exploit prevention
Explanation:

Secure Endpoint performs in-memory attack prevention through exploit prevention mechanisms, which detect and block attempts to exploit vulnerabilities in system memory to execute malicious code or activities.

370. A) One-to-one file protection
Explanation:

One-to-one file protection is the component in Secure Endpoint that helps to block files based on SHA-256 hashes or signatures, allowing organizations to prevent the execution of known malicious files.

371. C) MDM (Mobile Device Management)
Explanation:

MDM (Mobile Device Management) refers to the management of mobile devices within an organization, including tasks such as provisioning, securing, monitoring, and managing mobile devices to ensure consistent security and compliance.

372. C) Fuzzy fingerprinting
Explanation:

Cisco Secure Endpoint uses fuzzy fingerprinting to identify malicious files based on static attributes. Fuzzy fingerprinting involves comparing file attributes against known patterns of malicious behavior to detect potential threats.

373. C) Endpoint IoCs
Explanation:

Endpoint IoCs (Indicators of Compromise) provide a powerful threat-hunting capability for scanning post-compromise indicators across multiple endpoints. They help identify potential security incidents or breaches by flagging suspicious activities or behaviors.

374. B) Extension exclusion
Explanation:

An extension exclusion set excludes files with a specific extension from being scanned or flagged by security measures. This allows organizations to customize their security policies based on file types.

375. D) Data encryption.
Explanation:

Cisco Secure Endpoint's detection and protection features primarily focus on identifying and mitigating security threats on endpoints. While data encryption is an essential aspect of data security, it is not typically included as part of the detection and protection features of the Cisco Secure Endpoint. Instead, Cisco Secure Endpoint focuses on features such as anti-malware capabilities, indicators of compromise (IoCs) for threat detection, and dynamic file analysis for identifying and analyzing suspicious files and activities on endpoints.

376. C) By assisting with threat response and proactive threat hunting
Explanation:

Cisco Secure Endpoint helps with digital forensics and incident response (DFIR) by assisting with threat response and proactive threat hunting. It provides tools and capabilities to investigate security incidents, identify root causes, and take appropriate remediation actions.

377. C) To ensure secure access
Explanation:

The role of multifactor authentication (MFA) in endpoint security is to ensure secure access by requiring users to provide multiple forms of identity verification before granting access to sensitive resources or systems.

378. D) By using exploit prevention
Explanation:

Applications can be blocked from executing on endpoints using Cisco Secure Endpoint by using exploit prevention mechanisms. These mechanisms detect and block attempts to exploit vulnerabilities in applications or systems to prevent unauthorized execution of potentially malicious code.

379. B) Exploit prevention
Explanation:

Exploit prevention is the feature in Cisco Secure Endpoint that can prevent in-memory attacks on running processes. It detects and blocks attempts to exploit vulnerabilities in memory to execute malicious code or activities.

380. A) Endpoint indicators of compromise (IoCs)
Explanation:

Cloud-based pattern recognition in Cisco Secure Endpoint triggers more in-depth investigations when endpoint indicators of compromise (IoCs) are detected. These IoCs provide valuable insights into potential security threats or breaches, prompting further analysis and response actions.

381. B) Establishes a chain of custody for assets
Explanation:

One key benefit of having full lifecycle asset management in an organization is that it establishes a chain of custody for assets. This helps track the ownership, location, and status of assets throughout their lifecycle, enhancing accountability and security.

382. B) Loss or theft of mobile devices
Explanation:

One of the most common areas for asset risk mentioned in the text is the loss or theft of mobile devices. Mobile devices are often targets for theft, and

if lost or stolen, they can pose significant security risks, especially if they contain sensitive data or access to corporate networks.

383. B) Cisco Meraki Systems Manager
Explanation:

Cisco Meraki Systems Manager provides device management functionality to ensure consistent security across a variety of devices. It allows administrators to manage, monitor, and secure mobile devices, laptops, and other endpoints from a centralized dashboard.

384. B) Sentry functionality
Explanation:

Cisco Meraki SM includes sentry functionality to tag devices and enforce policies. This feature enables administrators to apply specific security policies or configurations based on device characteristics, such as device type, location, or user group.

385. C) Online brute-force attack
Explanation:

An online brute-force attack involves an attacker actively trying to log in to applications using many different combinations of credentials. The goal is to guess the correct username and password combination to gain unauthorized access to an account or system.

386. B) Offline brute-force attack
Explanation:

An offline brute-force attack is difficult to detect but requires a great deal of computational resources from the attacker. In this type of attack, the attacker attempts to crack passwords by trying many different combinations offline, often using powerful computers or specialized hardware.

387. B) A second source of identity validation
Explanation:

Multifactor authentication (MFA) requires a second source of identity validation beyond just a password. This could include something the user has (like a smartphone or security token), something the user knows (like a PIN), or something the user is (like a fingerprint).

388. B) Something you know
Explanation:

The common term for a single-authentication approach based on a password is "something you know." This refers to the user's knowledge of a secret, such as a password or PIN, to authenticate their identity.

389. A) A software token
Explanation:

A common form of the second source of identity validation in MFA is a software token. This is typically a mobile app that generates one-time passwords or codes that users must enter along with their password for authentication.

390. B) Man-in-the-middle attack
Explanation:

A man-in-the-middle attack involves an attacker intercepting communication between two sources and impersonating both parties. The attacker can eavesdrop on the communication, modify messages, or steal sensitive information without the knowledge of the legitimate parties involved.

391. C) Utilize multifactor authentication
Explanation:

A key recommendation to prevent ransomware exposure mentioned in the text is to utilize multifactor authentication (MFA). By requiring multiple forms of identity validation, MFA can help prevent unauthorized access to systems and reduce the risk of ransomware attacks.

392. C) Operating system patch checks
Explanation:

Posture assessments typically include operating system patch checks to minimize risk. Ensuring that operating systems are up-to-date with the latest security patches helps mitigate vulnerabilities and reduce the risk of exploitation by attackers.

393. B) Remotely wipe data or lock the device
Explanation:

MDM (Mobile Device Management) tools often provide the capability for administrators to remotely wipe data or lock lost or stolen devices. This helps protect sensitive information from unauthorized access and mitigate the risks associated with lost or stolen devices.

394. D) Active Directory group membership
Explanation:

Cisco Meraki SM's sentry functionality does not use Active Directory group membership to tag devices and enforce policies. While it can leverage various device characteristics for tagging and policy enforcement, it typically does not directly integrate with Active Directory for this purpose.

395. D) Time of day
Explanation:

Time of day is not a common variable for password strength. Password strength typically depends on factors such as length, complexity, and

frequency of use, but the time of day is not typically considered a relevant factor in password strength.

396. A) Mobile device management (MDM)
Explanation:

Mobile device management (MDM) tools provide visibility and security across a variety of mobile devices. They enable administrators to manage, monitor, and secure mobile devices, ensuring compliance with security policies and protecting sensitive data.

397. C) To create business email compromise (BEC)
Explanation:

A common goal of phishing campaigns targeting users is to create business email compromise (BEC). This involves impersonating trusted entities or individuals to deceive users into revealing sensitive information, transferring funds, or performing other actions that benefit the attacker.

398. B) To provide two sources of identity validation
Explanation:

Multifactor authentication (MFA) adds an extra layer of security by requiring users to provide multiple forms of identification to verify their identity. Typically, this involves providing two or more of the following: something the user knows (e.g., a password), something the user has (e.g., a smartphone or hardware token), or something the user is (e.g., biometric data like fingerprints or iris scans). The primary function of MFA is to enhance security by requiring multiple credentials for authentication.

399. D) Increased internet bandwidth
Explanation:

The United States Federal Bureau of Investigation's Internet Crime Complaint Center (IC3) provides recommendations to prevent ransomware

exposure, including backing up data and keeping backups offline, utilizing multifactor authentication, and updating and patching systems. However, increasing internet bandwidth is not a specific recommendation for preventing ransomware exposure.

400. B) Chain of custody for assets
Explanation:

Full lifecycle asset management helps organizations track the entire lifecycle of their assets, including procurement, deployment, maintenance, and disposal. One aspect of this is maintaining the chain of custody for assets, which involves documenting the possession, control, transfer, and disposition of assets from acquisition to disposal.

401. C) Directory harvest attack
Explanation:

A directory harvest attack is a type of cyber-attack in which an attacker attempts to determine an organization's naming convention for email addresses or usernames by sending multiple requests to the email server. The goal is to gather valid email addresses or usernames, often to use in subsequent attacks, such as phishing or brute-force attacks.

402. B) Adopt a cloud approach
Explanation:

By adopting a cloud approach for device management, organizations can ensure that devices can be updated and patched regardless of their connection to the network. Cloud-based device management platforms allow administrators to remotely deploy updates and patches to devices over the internet, eliminating the need for devices to be connected to the corporate network for maintenance.

403. B) To check the patching of operating systems and security software

Explanation:

Endpoint posture assessments are used to evaluate the security posture of endpoint devices, such as computers, smartphones, and tablets. One of the primary purposes of these assessments is to check the patching status of operating systems and security software installed on the endpoints. This helps ensure that devices are up to date with the latest security patches and updates to mitigate vulnerabilities.

404. B) Remotely wipe data or lock the device
Explanation:

Mobile device management (MDM) tools provide administrators with the capability to remotely wipe data or lock devices that are lost or stolen. This helps protect sensitive information from unauthorized access and prevents potential data breaches. Additionally, MDM tools may offer features like geolocation tracking to help locate lost or stolen devices.

405. C) Once known, they are no longer useful
Explanation:

Passwords are considered an ineffective approach to authentication because, once known or compromised, they can be used by unauthorized individuals to gain access to systems or accounts. Unlike other authentication factors like biometric data or hardware tokens, passwords can be easily shared, stolen, or cracked through various means, diminishing their effectiveness as a sole means of authentication.

406. B) Consistent security across devices
Explanation:

One benefit of cloud-based device management is that it provides consistent security across devices. By centralizing device management in the cloud, administrators can enforce security policies, deploy updates and patches, and monitor device compliance consistently across a diverse range of devices, regardless of their location or connection status.

407. D) Phishing attack
Explanation:

A phishing attack involves using deceptive emails, messages, or websites to trick users into revealing sensitive information such as login credentials, credit card numbers, or personal data. Phishing attacks often involve sending victims to fake websites that mimic legitimate ones, where they are prompted to enter their login credentials, which are then captured by the attacker.

408. B) Device management
Explanation:

Cisco Meraki Systems Manager is a cloud-based mobile device management (MDM) solution designed to manage and secure mobile devices, including smartphones, tablets, and laptops, across an organization. One of its primary functions is device management, which includes tasks such as device provisioning, configuration, monitoring, and security enforcement.

409. **C) A second source of identity validation**
Explanation:

Multifactor authentication (MFA) enhances the authentication process by requiring users to provide two or more forms of identification to verify their identity. In addition to the traditional password, MFA introduces a second source of identity validation, which could be something the user possesses (such as a smartphone or a hardware token), something inherent to the user (like biometric data), or a combination of these factors. This additional layer of security helps reduce the risk of unauthorized access even if the password is compromised.

410. C) A physical token
Explanation:

In the context of multifactor authentication (MFA), "something you have" refers to a physical object or token that a user possesses and can use to authenticate their identity. Examples of "something you have" include hardware tokens, smart cards, USB security keys, or mobile devices that generate one-time passwords.

411. C) Track and manage them
Explanation:

When new devices are made available to users, organizations should track and manage them to ensure proper provisioning, configuration, and security. This may involve registering new devices in an asset management system, applying security policies and configurations, and monitoring device usage and compliance with organizational standards.

412. C) Full lifecycle asset management
Explanation:

Full lifecycle asset management encompasses the entire lifecycle of an organization's assets, from acquisition and deployment to maintenance and disposal. This includes managing the chain of custody for assets, which involves documenting the possession, control, transfer, and disposition of assets from onboarding to retirement or disposal.

413. D) Encrypted or hashed passwords
Explanation:

In offline brute-force attacks, attackers attempt to crack passwords by systematically trying all possible combinations until the correct one is found. To perform these attacks, attackers typically need access to encrypted or hashed password databases, which they can then attempt to crack using specialized software or hardware.

414. A) Mail transfer agent (MTA)

Explanation:

A message transfer agent (MTA) is a piece of software used in an Internet message processing system (MHS). It is in charge of transporting and routing email messages from the sender's computer to the recipient's computer. An MTA's core platform is an exchange system with a client/server design.

A message transfer agent accepts incoming emails and routes them to specific clients/users. The MTA's primary job is to route incoming messages to the appropriate end-user or destination. Microsoft Exchange best shows MTAs, and UNIX sends mail.

415. B) Tagging devices to enforce policies
Explanation:

Cisco Meraki Systems Manager (SM) provides sentry functionality, which allows administrators to tag devices and enforce policies based on those tags. This feature enables the implementation of specific security measures and configurations tailored to different groups of devices or users within the organization.

416. B) Consistent security policies
Explanation:

One of the benefits of using Mobile Device Management (MDM) tools is the ability to enforce consistent security policies across all managed mobile devices. MDM solutions enable organizations to centrally configure and apply security settings, ensuring uniform protection against various threats and vulnerabilities.

417. B) Credential brute-force attacks
Explanation:

Multifactor authentication (MFA) enhances security by requiring users to provide multiple forms of identification before granting access. One of the threats that MFA helps prevent is credential brute-force attacks, where

attackers attempt to gain unauthorized access by systematically trying different combinations of usernames and passwords.

418. B) To provide identity validation
Explanation:

In authentication, the primary purpose of a password is to provide identity validation. Users provide their passwords as a means to confirm their identity and gain access to systems, applications, or resources that require authentication.

419. C) Patching of operating systems
Explanation:

Endpoint posture assessments typically check various aspects of endpoint security, including the patching status of operating systems and software applications. These assessments help ensure that endpoints are adequately patched and protected against known vulnerabilities and exploits.

420. B) Something you have
Explanation:

In Multifactor authentication (MFA), a common term for a second source of identity validation is "something you have." This could include physical devices like smartphones, tokens, or smart cards that users possess and use as additional factors to authenticate their identity.

421. B) Keep backups offline
Explanation:

One key recommendation from the United States Federal Bureau of Investigation's Internet Crime Complaint Center (IC3) to prevent ransomware exposure is to keep backups offline. Storing backups offline ensures that they are not accessible to ransomware attacks and can be used to restore data in case of an incident.

422. C) Exploits and eavesdropping attacks
Explanation:

A well-defined patch strategy helps prevent exploits and eavesdropping attacks by ensuring that systems and software are regularly updated with security patches to address known vulnerabilities. Patching vulnerabilities promptly reduces the risk of exploitation by malicious actors.

423. C) Man-in-the-middle attack
Explanation:

A man-in-the-middle (MitM) attack involves the attacker intercepting communication between two parties and impersonating both of them to gain unauthorized access to information or manipulate the communication. MitM attacks can occur in various contexts, including network communications and online transactions.

424. C) Enhanced security through additional identity validation
Explanation:

A primary benefit of multifactor authentication (MFA) is enhanced security through additional identity validation. By requiring users to provide multiple forms of identification (such as passwords, biometrics, or security tokens), MFA helps reduce the risk of unauthorized access, even if one factor is compromised.

425. B) Require complex passwords and change them regularly
Explanation:

To reduce the risk of password compromise, organizations should require users to use complex passwords and change them regularly. Complex passwords are harder for attackers to guess or crack, while regular password changes help mitigate the impact of compromised passwords.

426. **B) Operating system version**
Explanation:

A common check in a security policy for endpoints is verifying the operating system version. Ensuring that endpoints are running supported and up-to-date operating systems helps mitigate security risks associated with known vulnerabilities and ensures compatibility with security patches and updates.

427. **C) Full visibility and consistent security**
Explanation:

Mobile Device Management (MDM) tools provide full visibility and consistent security for mobile devices within an organization. They allow administrators to enforce security policies, manage device configurations, and monitor device usage to ensure compliance with organizational security requirements.

428. **C) Utilize MDM tools**
Explanation: The text recommends utilizing Mobile Device Management (MDM) tools to maintain security on mobile devices. MDM solutions provide centralized management capabilities for mobile devices, allowing organizations to enforce security policies, manage configurations, and protect against threats.

429. **C) Remotely wipe data or lock the device**
Explanation:

When an endpoint is lost or stolen, organizations should take immediate action to protect sensitive data by remotely wiping data or locking the device. This helps prevent unauthorized access to confidential information and reduces the risk of data breaches.

430. **C) The entire lifecycle of assets from onboarding to retirement**
Explanation:

Full lifecycle asset management includes managing the entire lifecycle of assets from onboarding to retirement. It involves processes such as asset acquisition, deployment, maintenance, tracking, and disposal, ensuring that assets are effectively managed throughout their lifecycle.

About Our Products

Other products from VERSAtile Reads are:

 Elevate Your Leadership: The 10 Must-Have Skills

 Elevate Your Leadership: 8 Effective Communication Skills

 Elevate Your Leadership: 10 Leadership Styles for Every Situation

 300+ PMP Practice Questions Aligned with PMBOK 7, Agile Methods, and Key Process Groups – 2024

 Exam-Cram Essentials Last-Minute Guide to Ace the PMP Exam - Your Express Guide featuring PMBOK® Guide

 Career Mastery Blueprint - Strategies for Success in Work and Business

 Memory Magic: Unraveling the Secret of Mind Mastery

 The Success Equation Psychological Foundations For Accomplishment

 Fairy Dust Chronicles – The Short and Sweet of Wonder

 B2B Breakthrough – Proven Strategies from Real-World Case Studies

About Our Products

CISSP Fast Track: Master CISSP Essentials for Exam Success

CISA Fast Track: Master CISA Essentials for Exam Success

CISM Fast Track: Master CISM Essentials for Exam Success

CCSP Fast Track: Master CCSP Essentials for Exam Success

Certified SCRUM Master Exam Cram Essentials

www.ingramcontent.com/pod-product-compliance
Lightning Source LLC
Chambersburg PA
CBHW060554060326
40690CB00017B/3709

9798328184427